My Chinese-America

Essays by Allen Gee

Library of Congress Cataloging-in-Publication Data

Gee, Allen.
My Chinese-America / Allen Gee.
pages cm
Summary: "Eloquently written essays about aspects of Asian American life comprise
this collection that looks at how Asian-Americans view themselves in light of America's
insensitivities, stereotypes, and expectations. My Chinese-America speaks on masculinity,
identity, and topics ranging from Jeremy Lin and immigration to profiling and Asian silences.
This essays have an intimacy that transcends cultural boundaries, and casts light on a vital
part of American culture that surrounds and influences all of us"— Provided by publisher.
Includes bibliographical references and index.
ISBN 978-1-939650-30-6 (pbk.)
1. Gee, Allen. 2. Chinese Americans—Ethnic identity. 3. Chinese Americans--Cultural
assimilation. 4. Chinese Americans—Biography. I. Title.
E184.C5G429 2015
973'.04951--dc23
                          2014026116

Published by SFWP
369 Montezuma Ave. #350
Santa Fe, NM 87501
(505) 428-9045
www.sfwp.com

Cover photo: John Farnan, "I Stand Witness"

Contents

"Profile" was previously published in *Gulf Coast*.

"Is It Safe There?" was previously published in a different version in *The Common*.

"Osaka" was previously published in *The Rio Grande Review*.

"Fraught With Masculinity" was previously published in *The Concho River Review*.

"Silences" was previously published in *The Newtown Literary Journal*.

"Point Guard" was previously published in *The South Loop Review*.

"Asians in the Library" was previously published in *THIS Literary Magazine*.

"The Real New South" was previously published in *Crab Orchard Review*.

"Echocardiography" was previously published in *The Portland Review*.

"My Chinese-America" was previously published in *Lumina*.

"By 2042" was previously published in *Solstice*.

Profile

I n mid-July during a summer when I wanted to remain in only one place, my mother called from upstate New York and asked, *Won't you visit? You aren't going to miss your father's sixtieth birthday, are you? And what about Matthew?* she reminded me, speaking of her first grand-child—my nephew—who was almost nine months old. *You should see him now. He's trying to walk, and you should hear him laugh. Can't you leave work for a while?* Hers was a selfless voice that strove to weave con-nections, that valued community and the continuity of tradition.

Listening to her, I recognized how much I missed her sensibility. I recognized how much she was expressing a desire to create or uphold what would last beyond death. This is what the Spanish philosopher, Mi-guel de Unamuno, in his essay, *Man of Flesh and Bone*, calls "the tragic sense of life". I have thought that my mother's Asian-American response to death, or her "tragic sense", was to invoke a constant plea for family.

Soon after my mother's call, I departed from the heat and humid-ity of Houston, Texas. I drove north with my girlfriend to the town of Granbury, where I left her so she could visit with her parents. The next day I continued north on Interstate 35 and reached Oklahoma. The verdant hills and ripe fields of the farmland were beautiful, serene; the pastoral landscape soothed my eyes. I kept heading north, and by early afternoon I reached Kansas. There the fields grew even wider, opening up and rolling on like expressions of infinity. The range of my vision was being tested with every glance, and I felt benevolently inspired to imagine the lives and the excitement of pioneers forging westward long ago. As I enjoyed the freedom and anticipation that so many Americans associate with traveling, I felt younger, somehow innocent. I felt very safe for a while. After heading northeast, I stopped for the night in the town of Emporia and looked forward to the rest of the scenic journey.

But the next morning, not twenty minutes up the highway I spotted a Kansas State Police cruiser waiting ahead on short grass. I was not speeding, but when the trooper pulled out and started to follow my pickup truck very closely, I couldn't help feeling at risk. He swerved out, shot ahead of me, steered onto the breakdown lane, and allowed me to pass. Then he abruptly swung back out and started to follow my truck again. I felt frightened, and any thought that I possessed the freedom to travel safely across the country quickly dissolved into a foolish notion. The trooper passed my pickup a second time and sped by a tractor-trailer, and although I passed the tractor-trailer and followed at a very cautious distance, the trooper immediately steered onto the breakdown lane and slowed once more. He waited until I passed by and then began to pursue me with flashing blue lights. As I sat stopped along the shoulder and felt every other motorists' eyes upon me, I watched the intense flashing blue lights in my rearview mirror and began to feel guilty. I started to believe that this incident was partly deserved, or entirely my fault, that I should never have left Houston and should have stayed there, tending to the relationship with my lover, living in my work, remaining in only one place.

Meanwhile, I had the trooper to contend with. To display the required compliance, I removed my registration and insurance card from the glove compartment and pulled my driver's license from my wallet. I held these items outside of my driver's side window while watching the side mirror for the officer's approach. When he reached my vehicle and leaned over, I saw he had short-cropped blonde hair and vigorous blue eyes. He was a shorter man; as if to compensate for his height, he had obviously lifted weights to add muscle to his chest and arms. I judged from his smooth face that he was younger than I, and I thought—what reason could there be for stopping me?

I'm sorry for all the flybys, he said, *but the first time I ran your license plate, nothing came back. I stopped you because you failed to use your signal changing lanes.*

I sighed and asked if he was going to give me a ticket.

No, he said, *I'm only going to give you a written warning. There's no fine or court appearance.*

Despite the absence of any anger or hostility in his voice, I didn't trust him. Then he asked, *Where are you headed?*

At this point, I still believed that there might not be any further problems. It had been established that I had committed no serious offense, and I held onto the idea that he might be able to see me for who I was. So I told him that I was a doctoral student who taught English and Asian-American Studies at the University of Houston. I told him that I was driving to Iowa and Ohio to visit some old friends before vacationing with my family in Albany, New York. Pointing to my bags, some fishing tackle, a boxed computer and printer in the truck's extended cab, I explained how I still needed to finish some research while on vacation. I spoke in a regretful voice, hoping that he might realize how I felt overworked and underpaid, as he probably felt. I wore a gray v-neck shirt, khaki shorts, Asics cross-training shoes, and polarized sunglasses. My haircut was short and neatly trimmed. I projected, by far, a clean and professional image. Between that and being a hard-working doctoral student en route to visiting my family, I exemplified the model minority.

But when the trooper returned to my driver's side window and handed me the written warning along with my license, registration, and insurance card, he did not admonish me to drive carefully and release me. *Allen,* he said in a deceptively amiable voice, *can I search your vehicle?*

I asked why. I was becoming angry. In the part of myself that has always tried to remain observant and rational, though, I knew that because of my out-of-state license plates and Asian features, and the fact that I was traveling from Houston to New York, he suspected I was delivering drugs. He answered my question with, *You're not in a hurry, are you?*

The Rodney King incident and the image of officers bludgeoning King with batons flew into my mind. I imagined being marched from the side of the highway and flung down into an irrigation ditch, then having the toe and heel of a black leather boot jammed into my spine. Or the trooper might radio for another trooper and fabricate a charge or plant drugs in my clothes or in my truck. As angry as I felt, and as much as I wanted to protest, I told him I wasn't really in a hurry, and I consented to the search.

I need you to sign a form, he said, and motioned for me to step out. In the next instant as I stood on the side of the highway, my eyes beheld the Kansas fields that had earlier inspired me to feel the freedom and anticipation of traveling; the speed at which that sublime feeling had vanished was profoundly disconcerting. I felt powerless and vulnerable. Contemplating that moment in retrospect, I have thought of Thomas Jefferson's writing in the beginning of *The Declaration of Independence* that "all men are created equal". I have not thought of how Jefferson intended for his famous phrase to be read, for he was addressing Caucasian males; rather, I have recalled Senator Charles Sumner's interpretation of Jefferson's famous phrase, since it was Sumner who, in 1802, insisted that Jefferson's words actually mean "all men", irrespective of race or color.

Certainly that morning in Kansas, when the trooper brought the form out and compelled me to sign it, he did not view me as being included in "all men." He viewed me as Roland Barthes' "Other." For I signified everything the trooper was not; from his perspective, I represented what is feared and thus exists to be conquered.

The trooper led me around to the passenger side door. *Start with the computer box*, he said. I asked if he expected me to pull off all the masking tape securing the top. *Yes*, he said and smiled.

Imagine the indignity of having one of the symbols or instruments of your life of learning set down on the side of the highway in the gravel and dirt to be inspected for illegal contents. Imagine the further indignity of being told to set the printer down on the side of the highway, followed by your luggage. I hated him for his covertness, for his cowardice, for not once voicing his suspicions. I watched in seething silence as he unzipped one of my Cordura travel bags—an old graduation present from my parents—and ran his hands, his fingers, between my folded T-shirts.

As he searched through the last of the T-shirts, I told him to pick it up. He did. On the front of the shirt was a print of stick-figure children of all colors with their hands linked; the words below them read: "Not one more. Making Children, Families, and Communities Safer From Violence." I asked the trooper to turn the T-shirt around. He saw on the back the emblazoned cartoon and national campaign figure of Mc-Gruff, the crime dog, and the slogan: "TAKE A BITE OUT OF CRIME 1-800-WE-PREVENT."

In an assertive voice, I told the trooper I wasn't the drug type

He ignored my remark and ordered me to open a tote bag. Inside he found Asics running shoes, quarter socks, DeSoto shorts and mesh tops. I told him that I ran 5K and 10K races and still lived partly like the athlete I had once been in high school. *What's in that bag?* he asked, pointing to another piece of my luggage. I opened my black, three-compartment shoulder bag that contained almost twenty hardcover books. Across the tops of the pages, each book bore the black ink stamp: University of Houston Libraries. After repeating that I was doing summer research, I asked the trooper if he imagined I would have time to sell drugs with so many books to read. His expression feigned indifference. He told me with an irritated voice to open a small knapsack. There were fishing reels and a few fly boxes; I remarked that whenever I had any real time off, I spent it on rivers or lakes, or down at the Gulf of Mexico, as far as possible from the city.

Your reels are nicer than mine, he said. He gazed at one of my fly rods and commented, *That's a fancy case*. His voice conveyed distance and resentment, as though it were difficult for him to perceive my becoming part of an aspiring middle class.

I asked him if he fished for largemouth bass and crappie, which are commonly caught in the Midwest. I told him I was going to do some fishing for channel catfish and flatheads on the Skunk River in southern Iowa for a few days, especially at night. I was still attempting to establish a human connection, despite how there has never been a shared history between Asian-Americans and European-Americans; despite how there have never been mutual alliances, but exclusion laws, internments, glass ceilings, restrictions based upon over-representation, and ever-evolving stereotypical images. Indeed, from Supreme Court rulings on immigration and citizenship, to the matter of hate crimes, there has not been a long or distinguished history of fairness, but only suspicion and a lack of trust between Asian-Americans and the law.

I was not surprised, therefore, when the trooper pointed to the truck bed and said impatiently, *I need to see what's in the toolbox.*

Tools, I told him, were all that he would find. Still he searched the box. After not finding anything, he clenched his jaw furiously and walked around to the tailgate, bent down on one knee, and inspected the spare tire stored beneath the truck bed. I told him that he shouldn't even bother getting his pants dirty. He wouldn't stop, though, so while he examined the tire, I rearranged my luggage.

Finally he emerged from beneath the truck. We stood facing each other, like farmers exchanging talk about the crops or the weather, with our hands resting on the sides of the truck bed. *It was because you were packed light,* he said, trying to justify his search. I heard scant regret and no apology in his voice, but that did not matter. I shook my head and told him—referring to a national television commercial that showed an egg being cracked and hissing in a frying pan, along with the slogan, "This is your brain on drugs"—that my brain wasn't on drugs and my best friend from high school was now a state trooper. *You should be on your way,* the trooper said, not open to hearing any of it. I walked back to my driver's side door, wanting very much to regain my composure for the rest of the long distance left to travel.

~

The hopeful and ameliorative side of me would like to believe that due to the scant regret I heard in the trooper's voice, and since I had talked fishing with him, that his judgments and expectations about me might have been altered. But I am certain that isn't what occurred; I feel confident that the trooper will still be waiting out on that lonely stretch of Kansas highway, determinedly stopping drivers for no real violations. His behavior, after all, exemplified that of the rugged individual who seeks conflict and lives by aggression. His response to the knowledge of death, his "tragic sense of life", causes him to seek heroic fame, to attempt to create his own legend, or to make—at all costs—the most significant drug arrests, so we might even see the story reenacted on television, on shows like *Stories of the Highway Patrol*. If he succeeds, his story looms so large that he will be remembered and acknowledged for years to come, a heroic figure whose deeds live far beyond the grave.

As for my own sense of self, two days beyond Kansas I woke early in the cold of morning and prepared to fish the Skunk River. Since we would be setting bank poles and trotlines on a remote stretch of shallow water, I asked my friend, Tony, if he thought I needed to buy a fishing license. *Don't worry*, Tony said. *The local game warden won't be out. He's old and fat. All he does is sit and drink coffee at the diner.*

I asked Tony if he was going to buy a license, or if he already had one.

No, Tony said. *Why bother?*

The sick feeling from the knowledge of how I could be viewed still resided within me. I thought about how common it was, how accepted it would be, for most men from that part of the country to see a Chinese-American fishing on their abundant river. I realized the judgment, the scrutiny I would provoke.

Although the delay would keep us from reaching the fishing camp at the most desirable hour, I directed Tony to drive to Iowa City. He tried to convince me of the innocuousness of the Skunk River and emphasized the sedentary habits of the game warden again, but I wouldn't budge. I insisted that we make a detour instead of heading straight to the river. We stopped at Paul's Discount Store, where I opened my wallet at the front counter and begrudgingly purchased my fishing license.

Some months later in September, I heard about the DWB, the Driving While Black or Brown bill proposed by Senator Kevin Murray of Los Angeles, California. The bill would have required the California Highway Patrol and major police and sheriffs' departments to record detailed information on the practice of stopping people on the basis of race, including the number of minorities searched and detained. I wondered how many California motorists might, like I, have preferred that it be a Driving While Black, Brown, or Yellow bill. I wondered how many "Americans" badly wanted for the bill to pass. When Governor Gray Davis vetoed it, he said that although he found so-called racial profiling "abhorrent", the DWB bill would cost too much and place too heavy a burden on law enforcement.

What burden? To be accountable for inordinate amounts of profiling?

Sumner's view of "all men" must thrive everywhere, whether in California or Kansas. Why shouldn't there be, for everyone, the freedom of traveling? What is a profile but a racial bias, a stereotype, or an attitude stemming from ignorance? I don't wish to feel cordoned off, to feel like I have to remain in one place, but for myself and many people of color with whom I have spoken, this is, for the time being, part of our being American. It is part of our sense of the shape of this democratic society.

We must envision and create something different, for none of us should be left patiently waiting.

Is It Safe There?

Two years ago I flew from where I live in rural Georgia to Chicago for a conference, and that Friday evening some Caucasian friends wanted to eat *dim sum* and asked if I'd take them to Chinatown. I suppressed a laugh, because my family usually only eats *dim sum* at lunchtime, not considering it as dinner fare. I found the circumstances even more amusing because although I'd never been to Chicago's Chinatown, my friends were bestowing a *de facto* authority upon me based on my ethnicity. One of my friends, noting that we would be visiting Chinatown at night, asked, "Is it safe there?" I realized he was envisioning a Hollywood stereotype, the sort of depiction stemming from a film like Roman Polanski's *Chinatown*. Polanski ignores the vibrancy of Chinatown as an ethnic neighborhood and pits middle-class hero Jake Gittes (played by Jack Nicholson) against ingrained corruption and streets filled with violent crime. It is this harsh view that is supposed to be intuited by the viewer as the predominant reality of Chinatowns everywhere.

I know, however, of the Chinatown, New York of long ago—not from the movies, but from my parents. My grandfather, like a grand impresario, decided to host their wedding reception there. They were married on September 19, 1959, and he personally invited everyone to the reception, stopping by at the Gee, Lai, and Gong Family Association buildings. Once invited, you could bring any number of family members; it was a matter of honor not to overstep the generosity of the invitation. Prior to the wedding, as a sign of respect, my grandfather provided my mother's family with moon cakes and slices from a suckling pig. I should add that the wedding reception lasted for three consecutive nights.

My parents told me about this when I was a teenager, their talk a prelude, setting the standard in my mind for what my own wedding should be like someday. Your culture, they were telling me, is elaborate and unique. Since a well-off family friend photographed the reception banquets in color, we possess pictures that were uncommon for the time; these photos have made my parents' expectations seem all the more explicit.

In a photograph of the nuptial ceremony, my father wears a white tuxedo with a black bowtie, flat-fronted black pants, and black leather shoes. My mother wears a white headpiece and fingertip veil, two strings of pearls, and her white full-length *peau de soi* wedding gown with a scoop neck and lace on top, the three-foot train hanging from her waist. But for the first night's reception on Saturday, she changed into a heavy brocade *cheongsam*, a one-piece body-hugging dress. The style had been made fashionable by Shanghai upper class in the nineteen-twenties; it was sewn from red silk and embroidered with birds and flowers, had a flat collar, sleeves covering her arms to the elbow, a hem just below the knee, and a slit revealing a very modest amount of skin.

On that first night—the evening designated for my parents "American" or white friends, the minister, and all of the out-of-town relatives—everyone gathered at the Toy Wan restaurant. The second night, my mother's *cheongsam* was silvery blue; on the third night, it was emerald green. Since my mother's father was a laundryman, and since laundries were closed on Sundays, the second night was reserved for laundrymen and their families. Two restaurants were needed to accommodate all of the guests, so a driver chauffeured my parents back and forth between Toy Wan on Canal Street and the Pacific restaurant on Mott Street. Since my grandfather worked in the restaurant business, and Mondays were traditionally their day off, the third reception at the Toy Wan had been designated for restaurant employees.

My mother and father have often reminisced about many of the dishes that were served during those three nights, the banquets requiring an intense level of preparation that has all but vanished in Chinatown kitchens across the country. For appetizers the waiters served shark's fin soup, bird's nest soup, dried oysters with abalone, diced chicken with cashews, and deep-fried stuffed mushrooms. What could be more impressive for a main course than winter melon soup, steamed and served in the whole melon itself? The melon's green skin was carved with intricate designs, the soup flavored with the meat of the melon, chicken stock, and a plethora of vegetables. Add to the menu red-cooked squab; gooey duck, first marinated before being deep-fried and then steamed; roast suckling pig; simmered chicken with ham and mustard greens; sea cucumbers with vegetables; fried rice; and noodle dishes, symbolic of longevity. Toward the end of the meal, the waiters brought out sweet almond drinks to prepare the palette for the dessert of red bean pudding. The wedding cake (only served on Saturday), frosted in whipped cream with pineapple, came from the Cottage Bakery on 33rd Street.

It's rare to hear of these extended celebrations anymore, because they're unaffordable. Yet this type of food, with its elaborate preparation, was once a regular feature of the rituals of life. Nowadays throngs of tourists crowd Chinatown's streets on the weekends seeking *dim sum*, which is less costly and far easier to make, but the standard is lower.

Hundreds of guests were invited to my parents' wedding receptions; the photographs reveal how vibrant and inclusive the festivities were, all the guests well-attired. What stands out the most, though, is the glowing expression of shared happiness; there is a genuine sense of *joie de vivre*, of Asian exultation. Everyone is smiling, white teeth gleaming as people talk and laugh animatedly, dining late into the night. When I finally married seven years ago in a backyard garden in Decatur, Georgia, the ceremony was lovely, and my parents were present and happy, but part of me silently regretted that there was no high Chinatown standard to have chosen from for the food, and the reception lasted for only one evening.

When I think of the Chinatown of my childhood, I recall always hoping there would be time to stop at the arcade on Mott Street called Chinatown Fair. The building's façade was dominated by glass doors that were left open in milder weather, beckoning the world inside. Upon entering, I became immediately surrounded by a child's play land of coin-operated rides, ski ball lanes, and a lunch counter that served ice cream sodas. Small prizes like cap guns or metal whistles under glass countertops tempted my eyes. High above, brightly-colored stuffed animals were displayed that could be won with tickets. My eyes were also always drawn to the mutoscope—a fortuneteller's machine—as well as a booth that contained a live dancing chicken. Still, I always gravitated first to the pinball machines lining the walls.

I played a Williams pitch-and-bat baseball game machine incessantly. As if my attention were an homage to assimilation, I stood absorbed, fascinated by how the silver steel ball popped out from beneath the pitcher's mound. My right hand reacted, pressing the button that swung the bat, which (when I was lucky) hit the ball, driving it up a ramp into right, center, or left field. I could have been Mickey Mantle or Joe DiMaggio playing for the Yankees; the arcade was a safe space where I was free to play and imagine. Indeed, if one peered closely enough, hundreds of individually finely-painted spectators could be seen in the pitch-and-bat machine's upper decks; for the cost of a mere dime, they were all watching me, cheering me on. I was the game's hero, never picked last, so I arrived each time with pockets filled with dimes.

The fortuneteller's machine frightened me; I watched others wait for predictions of the future from a turbaned figure with gleaming eyes, never wanting to know my own fate. But before leaving the Chinatown Fair, I always made my way toward the dancing chicken. The bird lived in a glass-fronted booth, and if you set a coin down in a metal slot and pushed a chrome handle forward, lights flashed, music played, and the chicken danced. It was supposed to be as carefree and entertaining as a vaudeville act, but my eyes had detected a wire metal grid that the bird was standing upon. I perceived, from how erratically the chicken moved, that it was not really dancing but hopping to avoid the small jolts of electric shocks. The cruelty struck me as shameless; I thought the arcade's owner should have been put in his own glass booth.

Although I'd been born in New York City, early on my parents, older brother, and I had moved upstate to Albany. Since my grandfather shared in the ownership of two Chinatown restaurants and other businesses, and since several of our relatives lived in Chinatown, my family was always driving down to New York for visits, so I spent many days there during my childhood. My grandfather used to take me along when he made his rounds to check on his restaurants and the other businesses. We always stopped at his favorite places; he led me through one doorway after another, proudly showing that he had a grandson, a legacy, as if our family would always be able to have a presence or a say in the community. The move upstate actually deepened the significance of being in Chinatown, because when I entered the arcade, I did not have to endure racist barbs or taunts like I did upstate—my childhood was my own, and I could imagine assimilating without cruelty, imaginary as it was, when I stood before the Williams pitch-and-bat baseball machine. Watching the dancing chicken, I thought I was like the bird, the jolts like the harassment I was enduring at my all-white schools. But in time, I became less drawn to the arcade, devoting myself more to playing contact sports, as difficult as competing physically against white classmates could be.

Eventually, the Chinatown Fair relocated from 7-9 Mott to 10 Mott across the street. Then, during the 1990s, the arcade became more of a haven for serious video gamers, and a few years ago I heard that a gutting and remodeling had left the arcade tamed and homogenized, resembling a Dave & Busters. By then, the effects of tourism were all too evident; the arcade had been renovated to serve outsiders rather than the Chinese who lived in the community. Not only was the old style arcade I had revered long gone, but the video gamers felt like their gritty space was ruined, having become a mass-market venue, an amusement center without a heart or soul. So I have not gone back to the Chinatown Fair, preferring to avoid seeing what has been done to the inside—that way, the arcade I knew will remain undisturbed, pristine, at least in my memory.

When my grandfather passed away in 1977, I was fifteen. His funeral was held at the Wah Wing Sang Funeral Parlor on Mulberry Street. The wake occurred in an inner chamber festooned with floral arrangements, and, as was customary, sour smelling incense was burned. Outside the chamber, on a small table, a silver tray offered quarters wrapped in white paper, the practice being that the sour incense emphasized one's need for sadness, but afterwards you should purchase some sort of candy to nurture a sweet remembrance, to keep from prolonged grieving.

When my grandmother, my parents, my two brothers, and I climbed into the lead black limousine behind the hearse, we rode first to the Gee Poy Kuo Family Association building on Canal Street. My grandfather had been one of the association's founding members, so the hearse stopped out front by the curb. The driver opened the back door and stood quietly, lingering, creating a long silence during which my grandfather's spirit could say a proper final goodbye. Next we proceeded to the China Noodle Co. on Walker Street, then to the Pagoda Theatre on East Broadway, then the Han May Meat Co. on Mulberry, and finally to the Great Northern Trading Co. and the Wo Hop restaurant on Mott.

What has stayed with me the most was when the hearse idled in front of the Wo Hop on Mott, for time froze. I felt as if I sat in a sealed chamber, like I could have been a fish gazing out from an aquarium, because while all of the Chinese upon the sidewalks paused, bowing their heads in a communal display of reverence, many of the white tourists gawked. As some stared with morbid fascination, others pointed fingers. The tourists' expressions of repugnance and disapproval seared into me, and I felt angry at how the rituals of our culture were being condemned by those who had not been invited to Chinatown. White people, in other words, were intruding upon what was sacred. I have since thought that Chinatown has to tolerate intrusion unlike almost any other community in America; what city or town—other than New Orleans—would willingly allow strangers to observe funeral processions in droves? How would any white community react if countless Asian strangers showed up at a burial and visibly expressed derision?

In 2000 at the age of thirty-eight, I accompanied my father to several board meetings at the China Noodle Co. For over two decades he'd been serving as the board of directors' secretary, a position my grandfather had held when he originally invested in the business in the 1940s. Now, however, China Noodle was closing, so I felt it imperative to take photographs and document the factory's existence.

All of the assembly line machinery appeared well maintained, but the thicker noodles China Noodle produced were no longer in high demand. Thinner, more fashionable noodles, like angel hair pasta, had become highly desirable. China Noodle still used real eggs, imparting its products with a genuine pale yellow color, but many restaurants and stores were now requesting brighter yellow noodles, requiring manufacturing with artificial dyes. When the noodle company's board had debated about whether to refurbish the assembly line or shut down, they discussed the option of selling the factory, and an adjacent lot that was being leased to a parking company. China Noodle's property had actually skyrocketed in value, because all Manhattan property was now at a premium; the former undesirable ethnic ghetto of Chinatown had become, in investors' eyes, a locus of opportunity. This seemed to be a first step, as if the community were on the verge of being made over into something like the French Quarter in New Orleans. How long would it be before I saw splashy brochures featuring Chinatown condos? How soon would the community be repackaged, perceived by others as a hip and favorable new destination, a trendy and exotic but navigable locale?

Since no one had previously been allowed to intrude upon the men at China Noodle as they worked, they were told my presence with a camera was for a historical project. Flour dust clouded the air, and the machinery rattled and whirred. I began by photographing a cast-iron mixing vat more than four feet wide with huge exposed gears. Sacks of flour and starch stacked on nearby pallets rose over seven feet. Next I focused on a giant rolling machine that resembled a printing press, the machine attached to a long, flat, metal table, and various cutting machines stood in a row nearby. Lastly, I photographed the packing tables covered with cardboard boxes, scales, plastic bags, and clear wrap.

Two men labored, folding wide, uncut sheets of noodles as they fed out of the rolling machine. I counted six men hovering over the packing tables. All of the men wore white pants, white short-sleeve shirts, and white hats. I was startled by one man who stood out because he was white. He had thick-framed black glasses and a long, gray, tangled beard. Though scrawny, he worked rapidly, filling his boxes with efficient movements while speaking in Cantonese to the other workers. Noticing my curiosity, my father said, "He's been here for over forty years." I nodded and began to consider what must have occurred for such a man to end up working in this place, wondering what it had taken for him to be accepted by all of the Chinese workers.

I have since thought that the white man at the China Noodle Co. represents part of the vitality of Chinatown that much of America does not want to acknowledge, for isn't Chinatown an economically self-sustaining immigrant community, not taking jobs, but offering them to others? I have also wondered if the company's board wouldn't have decided so readily to close and sell if outsiders hadn't been driving up Chinatown's property values and taxes.

These days, I fondly recall accompanying my grandfather on his self-appointed rounds, but as more and more of the Chinatown I knew vanishes, I have the sense that more of my own history is disappearing, and so part of my self seems to be winnowing away, like I am slowly being erased. I'm left feeling less and less connected to where I once felt the most culturally anchored and secure and alive.

We are constantly told that change is inevitable in life, but what happens when we have almost nothing left to return to?

James Baldwin, writing on Harlem's racial strife in *Notes of a Native Son*, pronounces, "To smash something is the ghetto's chronic need." Chinatown will never riot, though. Silence prevails amongst Asian cultures like a virtue. But when I consider that Chinatown's food is no longer the same, that the Chinatown Fair is essentially gone, and that many would prohibit Chinese funeral practices, silence ceases to be golden. And when I see a longstanding company's doors close, and see how others would like to buy up Chinatown and price it out of existence, I have to speak up. Others need to speak up now, too. The tourists will continue to visit in droves, as they should be able to, but they should be far less focused on gentrification. And so I have to ask: were there benefits from Chinatown's past ethnic segregation? Will the community be safer if it remains a place many are afraid to visit? Segregation, in its own unique way, has functioned as a preservative, but tourism now threatens the character of the neighborhood. Imagine Chinatown's street vendors and sidewalk produce displays being forced out, like a snide commentary upon the unpretentious appearance of the crowded streets. Indeed, how many cultural traditions, what meaningful rituals—how much of the community of Chinatown itself—will remain if outside interference is allowed to continue?

I told my friend who was fearful about journeying into Chicago's Chinatown that Friday evening, "We'll take a taxi straight to the restaurant." Using my Blackberry, I found a highly rated dining establishment in no time, and within minutes we shared two cabs that dropped us off at the Triple Crown on Wentworth Ave. As soon as we stepped onto the street, I smelled the unmistakable sweet fragrance of *cha siu bao*—roast pork buns—wafting through the air. Part of me immediately felt homesick for the Chinatown of my youth. I felt embarrassed at how emotional I could easily have become; I could have wept like a boy in front of everyone, since *cha siu bao* can't be found in rural Georgia. I managed to hold myself together as we filed upstairs into the Triple Crown. After I ordered *dim sum* in Cantonese for my friends, I couldn't let the opportunity of being in Chinatown at dinnertime fall prey to eating lunch fare. Noticing my longing expression, one of the waiters approached, so I asked if he could bring me a whole fish steamed in ginger, as well as steamed white rice. The waiter smiled, approving of how I wanted to eat heartily, knowing I had been appeasing my friends.

When the steamed sea bass was brought out, head and all, I invited my friends to share and asked for several bowls of rice. My friends were adventurous and ate with me, expressing their admiration for the fish. Still, it was not the same; I missed dining with my family and sharing our memories of past banquets and the various dishes that had been served; I vowed to myself to book a flight soon to New York. After finishing the meal at the Triple Crown, my friends and I strode out onto the sidewalk, and within thirty seconds, as if having been telepathically summoned, two cabs appeared. We were whisked back uptown, as safe as ever, to the comfort of our convention hotel.

From my perspective, Chinatown was not a place to be feared at all; rather, it was a place to be revered, a place that needed to be protected from outsiders. So my mind began hurtling into an inverse mode of thinking. I wondered how my white friends would react if I asked them, each time we went someplace new where Caucasians are the distinct majority, for reassurance that I would be all right.

Osaka

When we first met at a trendy Houston hair salon called Hot Tops, I was oblivious that Niki had taken any real notice of me. We were sitting in the waiting area thumbing through glossy magazines. *I work in the cosmetics industry*, was all I later recalled hearing her say. But the next time we ran into each other at a happy hour in Montrose, she asked, *Would you like to have dinner at Osaka?*

The invitation startled me. Niki was much younger—twenty-two, I soon discovered—while I was thirty-seven. I paused, gathering myself, like someone learning to dive standing upon a high board staring down at glimmering water. As she stood looking intently at me, my impression was that she probably wasn't seasoned or wise enough, but she spoke with an earnest and deliberate resolve. This was no joke—why me, though?

In the superficial world of appearances, Niki was one of the beautiful people, whereas I resided, at best, on an average tier. It wouldn't have surprised me if she modeled for a living, but my inherent shyness and anti-chauvinist beliefs had caused me not to stare at her—she had only registered in my mind as someone young and thin. Indeed, I'd largely dismissed her when at the hair salon, because the women I typically sought were my own age or slightly older, and I preferred intellectual, nerdy, artistic types.

Niki reacted to my current hesitation, however, with the most refined and seductive pout of her mouth, followed by an admonishment with her eyes, communicating that the proposed date would be highly memorable, an event that I would not be able to forgive myself for later if I turned it down. Her whole expression read like a poignant exclamation: Are you afraid? Do you have any idea what you'll be missing? She challenged me with sexual innuendo, calling my masculinity and age into question.

How about next Friday? I asked.

During the week I pondered how Niki was white and I was Chinese-American. One Asian woman I'd gone out with had chided me for majoring in English and not keeping up with my Cantonese; I had learned from this more-Asian-than-thou experience that falling in love with a culture nationalist was probably impossible. Besides, I'd always dated women from all races, never wanting to acquire any fixed beliefs, as if my emotions belonged to an enlightened sphere on the level of liberal nirvana. Yes, what should race have to do with my love life? Nothing could be more hypocritical than my being a minority but falling prey to stereotyping. Considering that Niki was twenty-two with uncommon good looks, I wondered if I were clinging too much to mundane notions about age and beauty. What the hell. It was only a date, wasn't it?

Every date can be perceived as a journey, a miniature drama, though. We reveal who we are and allow ourselves to be judged. But what other way can we best determine if someone else is suitable? And can't a date be like alchemy or the equivalent of uncapping a well? The proposed Friday arrived, and as Niki strode into Osaka, I let myself observe her more closely. She possessed an irrefutable long-legged allure; she moved with the grace of someone who belonged in a photo shoot. Her face was striking: she had green eyes that gleamed, conveying an unusual energy and liveliness, seeming magical, like she hailed from Oz's Emerald City.

Her distinct cheekbones, refined nose, small jaw line, and delicate ears gave the impression of an elegant bird. She had an Aubrey Hepburn-like quality—magnetic, irresistible, inevitably drawing one nearer. Her slender proportions also intrigued me; I could imagine us running together in 5K races.

I could picture Niki elsewhere too: sleek in a black leotard, a lithe dancer bounding across a stage, or ice-skating across a frozen pond, gliding smoothly before leaping and twirling in the air.

Even sitting down she carried herself with perfect posture, staying noticeably upright, her shoulders level, back straight; she had the poise of a princess or a queen. In contrast, having finished doctoral studies a few months before, I slumped and resembled the classic introvert, my head more often than not bent over with my face stuck between the pages of a book, my mind always elsewhere, drawing parallels between novels or composing jazz riffs in the clouds of my thoughts. Yes, I was more likely to be taken for an absent-minded dreamer or some kind of brainy geek.

Again I wondered, I wanted to know: what had she ever seen in me?

We sat at a small square table on the main floor, within earshot of other customers. The waiter was a young Japanese man who smiled as if he were rooting for me to cross racial lines and succeed with seduction. When he asked for our drink preferences, we each requested hot tea and water. When he returned with a little steaming blue clay pot, two matching round mugs, and two clear water glasses, Niki asked if I would order dinner for her. She instructed me not to be tame, because she'd eaten all kinds of sushi before.

I ordered salmon and tuna hand rolls and nigiri (separate pieces over compressed rice), requesting yellowtail, halibut, eel, squid, and red snapper. Would Niki be put off by eating a lot because of how thin she was? Listening to the order, she showed no signs of being gastronomically inhibited. Once the waiter had veered off, she said boldly, not lowering her voice whatsoever, *I want to get to know you. I think you might have been shy growing up, but you've grown out of it some. How am I doing so far?*

She was partly correct, especially about my shyness, which had made dating infrequent. And I had outgrown some of my shyness from standing at the front of classrooms teaching, and because of a few long-term relationships. I was surprised by how loudly she'd just spoken—without any reserve. The volume raised the eyebrows of several customers at nearby tables. I would have preferred that my personal life, even in public among strangers, remain private. I attributed her bold delivery to youth, though, and since I was older and obviously not her type, part of me felt flattered by her effusiveness. What did it matter if most of the restaurant knew now that we were on a date?

You're doing fine, I said.

You grew up shy, she said, *but from an early age, I had to deal with too many boys. The first time I made out with someone, I was twelve. You aren't going to believe how it happened.*

Before I could comment on whether I wanted to hear about adolescent sex or not, she continued, *I was at a party with other kids from my junior high school. We were playing spin-the-bottle. When I spun, the bottle pointed to Jeff, and he led me into a closet. Instead of kissing me for a little while, he told me that he had the biggest crush on me. Then he kissed me once, and longer, and although I'd never considered him as a boyfriend, I liked it. So I let him keep kissing me. Soon we progressed to French kissing, which really wasn't too awful because he had a pack of wintergreen Lifesavers. Do you know that if you crush a wintergreen Lifesaver between your teeth in the dark, you can see tiny sparks? Jeff showed me. It was true. My friends couldn't believe how long we stayed by ourselves, and by the time we came out, the party was half over. We were talked about for weeks! What about you?* Niki stared inquisitively like I was a laboratory subject and she was a researcher in a white coat with a clipboard, recording precise findings based upon the levels of my responses. *When did you first kiss someone?*

You wouldn't believe it.

Try me, she said, daring me with a white smile that would have been perfect in a toothpaste commercial.

I had never gotten to know anyone on a first date by sharing stories about first kisses. I would have felt uncomfortable talking about the awkwardness of pre-teen sexuality, wet dreams, or raging hormones. But Niki waited, tossing her thick strands of lustrous black hair over her left shoulder, her green eyes as serious as a jeweler on the verge of splitting a diamond. It was as if she firmly believed, as a matter of principal, that I would be intrinsically better off for talking to her about my past.

My first kiss was in sixth grade also, I said, *but it was during an overnight trip to New York City. They actually let the entire junior high student council travel by charter bus down to New York and stay at a Ramada Inn. There were only two chaperones for over thirty students.*

Niki appeared rapt, listening attentively like I was a witness and she was a deposing lawyer.

We weren't supervised, I continued. *After a day of sightseeing, the chaperones just stayed in their rooms watching television. Who knew? Maybe they were having an affair. Whatever they were doing, that first Friday night all the students started calling each other. None of us wanted to stay cooped up in our rooms. Three eighth-grade girls telephoned, asking if I'd visit them, so I took the elevator and ran down the hallway to their room. They said they thought I was cute and they wanted to kiss me and would teach me if I didn't know how. So I made out with Mary, Lisa, and Susan. They passed me around for over an hour. They didn't even ask to play spin the bottle. I couldn't believe it, and I thought no one was ever going to believe me. It was the best field trip of my life.*

Did you ever see them again?

Whenever we passed each other in the hallways at school during the rest of the year, they smiled. But then they graduated and were gone. In high school two of the girls were on the cross-country team, so I saw them when I joined the team as a freshman. They were juniors by then. They were always kind to me, but as far as dating or ever being close to them again, it was as if their kissing me had never happened.

Did you feel ruined or used?

No, I was always glad for what happened. I wondered why Niki was making more of what had occurred when I hadn't confided about a problem. Was she looking for abuse because she'd been a victim? Wariness surged through me. I'd had no preconceptions about the date but certainly didn't expect it would be like this. The waiter brought our sushi out with chopsticks wrapped in white paper, and he smiled again like he was encouraging me to do whatever was necessary. By any means. As if we were Asian soul brothers bonded by the common goal of our racial oppression and therefore committed to infiltrating the white race.

I inhaled a long, calming breath, feeling relieved once he left.

Niki and I started nibbling on salmon hand rolls, but she kept talking. *By the time I was thirteen, I was sneaking off and making out with older boys in cars. I told my parents I was going to friends' houses to study, but I would be out on dates or at movies or parties. There was a lot of smoking and drinking, and the first time a boy talked me into sitting in the backseat with him, we had been drinking beer. I was fifteen. Everyone bragged about having sex while parking, but I didn't lose my virginity in a car.*

I nearly choked on the sushi I was eating, coughing until my throat was clear, my appetite suddenly gone. Niki stared at me like she expected for me to be reverently quiet, and I wondered if she realized that I didn't want to hear the story I thought she was going to tell. I wondered if my reluctance too hear it was too old-fashioned and conservative. Wasn't her generation raised to be more sexually open? I wondered if she would continue on that topic or intuit that I would prefer to get to know her another way. A middle-aged woman at the next table over stared at me with the most sympathetic look. Her face reddened; she appeared to be embarrassed for me, obviously having heard everything Niki had said.

I was a junior in high school, Niki said. *I was with my date after a fall dance. We hadn't been together long, but he was nice, and his parents were away for the weekend. We went to his house and started making out in his living room. Next there was some heavy petting. I wanted to have sex with him, so I pulled his clothes off and jumped him. He was a virgin, too, and he had no idea that it was going to happen. It was awkward at first, but once we realized what we could do, it was something. We did it twice, and ever since I've always liked to take the lead. I think of it as owning my own sexuality. It's who I am, so I'm proud of it. What about you?*

What about me? I felt trapped in the Bermuda Triangle of dating, ensnared, caught in an inescapable net; I hoped someone would appear out of nowhere and miraculously save me. Had I been more of an open book, I would have explained that my sexual history was varied, dependent upon the type of woman I was dating and the combination of physical, psychological, and emotional chemistry. I might have admitted that these days when I went on dates, women asked what was wrong with me, trying to establish why I wasn't married yet. My answer was always, *I haven't met the right person.* To sweeten the pursuit, or for those who liked a challenge, I would never admit to being lonely, only saying that as a writer, I didn't mind being alone, often preferring solitude. *If I'm going to be with someone,* I would say, *it's entirely by choice.*

Several women at the closest table had stopped talking now, as if any conversation they were sharing amongst themselves couldn't compete with what Niki had asked, or they were stunned into silence by how embarrassed they thought I must have felt.

What's the longest relationship you've ever been in? I asked.

Three months, Niki answered.

I saw that as a warning sign and didn't reveal that my relationships had lasted from two to three years, with marriage almost occurring twice. I didn't say that my first love was someone in college I hadn't had sex with but should have, and that I'd never stopped regretting how distance—my leaving for graduate school halfway across the country, and my not realizing how much I was in love—had caused me to lose her. I also didn't speak about how the loss of my virginity was something I hardly considered anymore, or that my last relationship over the span of two years had been the most sexually imaginative and involved one of my life.

I lost my virginity when I was a teenager, I said. I should have waited until I was in love. Anyhow, the first woman who I fell deeply in love and had sex with betrayed me. She left me for an older man who drove a Corvette, insisting he had real ambition, so she didn't feel guilty about cheating on me. He dumped her after a week, and then she begged for my forgiveness, trying to convince me she'd been deceived so none of it could be her fault. Of course, I couldn't listen to any of it. The damage had been done, so I'd already moved on.

That's really interesting, Niki said.

Why don't we eat a little? I suggested, gesturing at all the pieces of untouched sushi before us.

The way Niki had asked, *What about you?* echoed loudly through my thoughts. I remembered being fourteen when I was a freshman in high school. After I mentioned a girl I was dating to my father, he had said, *Is there anything I need to tell you now about sex?*

We had been sitting at the kitchen table. Dinner was already over. My mother was there, too. I had nearly burst out laughing but also felt sorry for my father. Did he actually think he had to have this talk with me *now?* My parents had probably discussed what direction they thought my life was taking since I'd been staying out late, but sex had never been even remotely discussed in our house, as if no one was or ever could become a sexual being. The seriousness of my father's voice, though, startled me a little. Was the underlying factor for his concern the fear that I could get a girl pregnant? That I might ruin my life? *Please,* I said, *don't say another word. I learned everything in Health class. The teacher even forced us to ask questions.*

In reality, my health class had laughed nervously as the teacher tried to maintain a serious discussion, and the material about having sex had seemed out of date, lacking any contemporary relevance. Still, I didn't want to give my parents any cause for anxiety. *You don't have to talk to me now about sex,* I insisted, whereby my father looked relieved, grateful that I was providing him with an escape from the most dreaded of parental obligations. He would probably have rather paid bills, and by that point I was imagining how awkward it would be to have to hear him explain birth control or sexual intercourse. Since he was a civil engineer, it would have been like listening to him read an automotive instruction manual.

I had one other related discussion with my parents during high school, when they told me about how they'd met, dated and married. They'd attended the Bronx High School of Science. Prior to turning sixteen, my mother had been the recipient of several marriage proposals from Chinese parents and suitors, but she'd been on only two dates. My father had also been on only a few dates. The first time they met, my father asked my mother out immediately, and after a long courtship, when they were twenty and twenty-one years old, they married and had been together ever since. In other words, they weren't experienced when it came to the complexities of dating. Notwithstanding, my mother had cautioned when I was seeing one particular girl who had a wild reputation, *You'll be better off if you wait until you're married to become physically serious with someone.*

As astounded as I was by the bluntness of her remark, I reassured her, *I know why you're worried. I promise, no unplanned pregnancies.*

You're not listening. You should at least be in love, my mother pressed.

I'll remember that, I said, and nodded respectfully.

Now, as Niki and I ate, she stared at me as if wanting to create an intimacy between us with her eyes, attempting through telepathy or the power of mental suggestion to instill sexual longing into my subconscious. *Do you know why I like Asian men more than others?* she asked.

There could have been the whine of a saw cutting into my brain. I felt like any possibility for the date's success was being relegated to the cold void of infinite space; she was venturing into unforgiving territory. *What makes you like Asian men?* I asked, wondering what she could possibly say.

Every white guy I've met has been more interested in my looks than who I am. Some have even been too forceful. I've been pushed more than once for not acting like I was supposed to. But I've never been treated badly by an Asian guy. They're generally nicer. And I like how much cleaner Asian men are. They have less hair.

I couldn't believe I hadn't realized it: Niki was an Asiaphile. She wasn't interested in me as much as the idea of me, of what she thought I was or could be, based on the hue of my skin and the shape of my eyes. Now the implications of our being at Osaka were forever altered; the restaurant choice probably didn't mean she was cosmopolitan and inclined to be an adventurous diner or world traveler, but that the percentages for landing suitable male targets increased exponentially provided she frequented an Asian specific locale. Or, maybe she just liked the vibe of being surrounded by Asians. Who knew? Anyone Asian who's been stared at by white people while eating with chopsticks—anyone who's been the object of the Orientalist gaze—knows what I'm suggesting.

The name of the restaurant—*Osaka*—became seared into my memory. Suddenly I wanted to be anyplace else, and I thought Niki had probably been very lucky, since if she kept on dating Asian guys, she couldn't continue to beat the odds. Someone would be cruel or domineering. No racial group, I could say with a vast certainty, had a monopoly on treating women better or worse.

I felt numb, disappointed, like I'd opened six different boxes, and each one contained a smaller one, but upon reaching the last box, I discovered that it was empty, without any treasure or gift inside. Niki's beauty was captivating and invigorating; she was a veritable fountain of youth, but I'd hoped that she was less enamored with her looks than the rest of the world and had gone to great lengths to emphasize substance. More than anything I wanted to be involved with someone intelligent and fun, a companion who would challenge and intrigue me. As much as Niki had been talking about her sexuality, and although sex would be very important for as long as I had a pulse and breathed, it was only a part of what I deemed important in a relationship.

I set my hands on the table and looked up at her. Our eyes connected. As I spoke, my voice sounded as condemning as an eighteenth century monarch. *I don't have any racial preferences.*

Knowing she was losing my interest, Niki challenged me, saying, *When I'm attracted to a man, I sleep with him on the first date. Do you know what that means?*

Silence enveloped the nearby tables; every customer became quiet. One young woman held her hand up to her mouth, and her face conveyed an oh-my-God expression. Niki didn't care, calmly ignoring the after-effects; her eyes saw me alone, and for a few seconds I nearly felt like we were the only ones there at Osaka, on the planet, or in the universe.

She was offering me what men were supposed to fantasize about. Not long before, a friend had told me that as his grandfather was dying, one of the last things the older man had said was, *If you're single, don't ever turn down a woman who says she wants to have sex with you. You'll live to regret it.*

My thoughts whirled. Wasn't Niki's aggressiveness, aside from being the type of offer that normally only occurred in alcohol commercials, an example of pure and unrepressed desire, uncensored and without hindrance? Shouldn't I have been admiring her audacity?

I refrained from revealing to her that she was making me recall how my parents had raised me. Was I still my parents' son? What—assuming that there was no risk of sexually transmitted diseases—did I believe in? My mother's words floated up through the folds of my brain, nudging against the present. *You should at least be in love.* Was Niki making me realize I was more of an old-fashioned romantic? I admitted to myself that my mother had been right—not for when I was teenager, but for who I was now. I still liked some mystery, the opportunity to get to know a woman before I learned all about her sexually. But would my being that way cause me to miss out on desirable women like Niki? Was I conforming somewhat to the stereotype of being less aggressive, or generally nicer, like the kind of Asian she had believed I was?

I waffled between feeling attracted to Niki and reminding myself that I barely knew her. Hesitation gripped my speech—I wasn't comfortable leaping into bed with any woman, Asian enthusiast or not. The waiter hastened over to clear the table and asked if we wanted dessert. We declined, and he strode off to the cash register and then returned with the check, smiling, urging me on one final time.

Do you know how many relationships I've had? Niki asked.

When I didn't respond, she said, *Nineteen. But I haven't fallen deeply in love. I really want that.*

I took out my wallet and paid, and Niki's eyes became anxious, expectant. *Where's the riskiest place you've ever been with a woman?* she asked.

My unspoken answer was: up in the Adirondack Mountains beside Pharaoh Lake, along a trail where we could have been discovered by any number of hikers. I had been with my last lover, whom I still missed constantly, but I wasn't about to reveal that to Niki or anyone else.

We pushed back our chairs, and Niki stared at me, entreating me again with her insistent eyes. As we emerged from the restaurant into the cool evening air, streetlamps flickered on, and Niki said, *My place isn't far from here.* She grabbed my hand and squeezed it, like she was guiding me resolutely, rewarding me because I'd been "nice".

So when I turned to face her and looked straight into her eyes, I felt bad. *I enjoyed dinner,* I said, *but I need to go home. I have to meet some people early in the morning at Memorial Park for a run.*

There seemed to be no easy way to tell Niki that for me, being older meant not settling, but waiting and being patient for the right woman. The right *one*. If a date felt off, I wasn't about to falsely encourage anybody and certainly not myself. There also seemed to be no way to tell Niki that she was right for someone, and that someone would have to be a nice guy, but I wasn't that guy. Was I sane, though? Turning her down after she'd offered what most men could only dream of? How vulnerable had she felt? I wondered if she behaved this way all the time, or had she been acting older and more sophisticated for my sake?

The realization that I wasn't going to be submissive on her behalf angered Niki; she huffed and glared downward like she could have spat on my shoes. Her mouth opened like she was about to insult me, but then she broke away, separating herself from me, obviously hurt, retreating quickly. The rescuer in me regretted rejecting her and almost called out, "Niki, wait," but then she was unlocking her car door and climbing into the driver's seat, so the chance to say anything had evaporated like mist after a rainstorm. Watching her drive off, I hoped she wouldn't be hurt.

More than once I thought about calling Niki to explain why we wouldn't have been a good match. I stopped myself each time, though, because of how abruptly she'd left me in the parking lot. I didn't imagine I'd ever see Niki again, but two months later, while entering a bistro for lunch with a friend, there she was. My friend was a painter with whom I wasn't at all romantically involved; she had wanted to meet with me to discuss the implications of working as a minimalist versus maximalist while creating abstract art. Niki glanced up from another table as I was sitting down; she was accompanied by a much younger man, and he wasn't Asian.

I waved to avoid seeming rude, but Niki gazed at me with a mournful, hurt expression that exclaimed, *How could you?* As if I were betraying her by having lunch with someone else. As if it were my fault she was with someone Caucasian.

Her eyes kept accusing me of cruelty, but I felt like we inhabited entirely different worlds. The frailty just beneath the surface of her boldness was all too palpable; I felt sad because all of this was the result of one invitation, one date, and one—my—rejection. The realization occurred that neither of us had turned out to be whom the other one had thought we were. Had I entirely destroyed her idealization of Asian men? Apparently so. Had she confirmed that I was an old-fashioned romantic? Older and needing to trust someone and fall in love, exactly as my mother had advised? That seemed to be the difficult truth.

Love felt impossible, elusive. I was thirty-seven but hadn't yet found a woman I wanted to marry. With each failed attempt came more reluctance to risk rejection, and for the next three years I'd be alone, wondering if I'd ever find anyone. *If.* Not *when.* Still, I felt genuinely sorry for Niki. Her accusatory look wouldn't subside from my memory, lingering on long after our doomed date. But she was much younger—she had years ahead of her that were behind me—and I wish I could admit having felt sorry for myself, too, but that would be much too revealing for a writer who preferred his solitude.

Fraught With Masculinity

Late one evening two and a half years ago in Milledgeville, Georgia, I glanced up from the checkout counter within the mind-numbing sprawl of a Wal-Mart, only to see over two dozen brazen youths from rival gangs swaggering through the aisles. They were shouting obscenities at each other while making their way toward the exit, heading outside *en masse* to fight. My wife had sent me to buy formula for our infant daughter, and since I was a dutiful new father, the request had triggered my provider instinct. I could have run over anything in my way.

All I needed to do was take a few steps to the right, turn left, exit through the sliding glass doors, reach my Dodge Dakota, and drive home. But the cashier rang up and bagged the formula slowly. So when I finally started to leave and headed to the right, both gangs were there, blocking my way out. As one of the gang member's sharp eyes dared me to cut in front of him, and as my eyes stared him down, the moment evoked several other times in my life—charged, potentially dangerous, fraught with masculinity.

While growing up in the 1960s, I had searched with a detective's diligence, but aside from Bruce Lee (who would die tragically young in 1973 at thirty-two), the visual landscape of America didn't offer many strong Asian-American role models. The martial arts vein held little appeal for me; I was impressed by but couldn't see myself executing jaw-snapping roundhouse kicks or delivering lightning-fast flurries of nearly invisible punches. Nor could I hear myself letting out guttural death growls or scaring anyone off with combative *hi-yahs*.

What I intuited before the age of twelve was how American representations of Asians failed to correspond with who I was, and aside from the dearth of role models throughout popular culture, Asian-American male stereotypes were already prevalent. Whether it was the mathematics geek, the youthful music prodigy, the fumbling Asian nerd who can't speak English properly or pronounce his Rs, or the ubiquitous older eunuch-type figure—in films or on TV, no matter who the actor was or the context of his role, Asian males were constantly emasculated to the extent of creating a nationwide mythology about smaller penis size. You understand just how powerful stereotypes are when your first girlfriend in your late teens tells you with breathless approval that you're not how she expected you to be.

Another reason the pervasive notion of Asian male emasculation lacked any truth for me was that my grandfather and father were such strong men. Steady providers, they'd never failed to take care of their families. My grandfather ran several restaurants in New York City and was known amongst other Cantonese as "the tall man". Like many Asians, my father ended up studying engineering in college, but he'd grown up playing stickball in the streets as a youth, was never bullied, and served as president of his high school class and his college fraternity. Despite this contradicting reality, I'm not at all surprised that Wesley Yang poses the question in his essay, *Paper Tigers*: "Why does it seem that so many Asians are so readily perceived to be, as I myself have felt most of my life, the products of a timid culture, easily pushed around by more assertive people, and thus basically invisible?"

In 1976, I competed in one of my first high school freshmen cross-country races at Central Park in Schenectady, New York. Virtually every runner except me was white. At one point, the course funneled into a narrow stretch between trees and traversed a wide ditch. Everyone started colliding, being crammed into the thin passage, and many fell to the ground. Fear swept through me, and I felt horrified watching how everyone kept running, trampling those who had been knocked down. Extending my elbows to create my own space, I ran cautiously and managed to avoid stepping on anyone. Those being trampled in the ditch were crying out like orphaned animals. Suddenly I felt someone grab at my right shoulder like he wanted to fling me to the ground and use me as leverage to keep himself upright. I shoved him away, defending myself, and repeated in my mind, "Don't stop." I felt unusually aggressive, but it was as if I'd been granted a glimpse into the reality of mental toughness. Perhaps I could determine my own fate amongst other males by willing my body to endure, using physical strength to survive. As I finished the race intact and staggered through the chute, my coach asked, "Are you alright? It was bloody out there. How did you make it?"

"I stayed tough," I answered, gasping for air, the realization setting in that struggling against others was psychological. And what I'd read about Darwin's theory of the survival of the fittest suddenly felt very pertinent and real, all too applicable to my own life.

In the summer of 1979, on a playground basketball court in downtown Albany, an African-American newcomer sneered at me and jeered in front of everyone, "Yo, China. What makes you think you can run here?"

He was thin and lanky and three or four inches taller than I. He had a close-cropped Afro and an oval-shaped face with a high forehead, prominent cheekbones, and a square jaw, but I was broader with more muscle in the chest and arms. I stared back dismissively, not speaking, because it would have been futile to explain that I was a regular, or to assert that I had been playing on that very court since I was fifteen, and that I'd never seen him before, so who was he to question my presence?

Yes, I felt wary, but I couldn't let him humiliate me; if anyone believed I could be intimidated, my chances of winning would be ruined—I would be a marked man—and why play then? So the first time that the new-comer drove on me and tried to score with a lay up, I leapt high and slammed the ball, sending it caroming off the metal backboard. The twanging noise echoed ominously, and the newcomer was totally un-prepared for the blatant physicality of my defense; he appeared startled by my forcefulness. "Yo, Africa," I said. "You want some more?"

All the regulars who knew me laughed, mocking how badly he'd un-derestimated me. I regretted having to be forceful with another minority, but he'd threatened my standing, challenging my right to belong. To my relief, he seemed to sense, as the game resumed, that a fight would only lead to further humiliation; he stayed quiet, sulking as he ran up and down the court. Since then, I have discerned that while emasculation is how Asian-American males are otherized, hyper-virilization and being attributed with a menacing intent to elicit fear is how African-American males are most often stereotyped. Neither minority group is allowed to be thought of as "normal"—that would deem them equal with whites.

In August 1993, at the age of thirty-one, I arrived at the University of Houston to study and soon located a one-bedroom apartment to rent on Berthea Street. The entire brick complex gave off a 1960s communal chic feeling—all the units were graced by old wood floors, high ceil-ings, generous large windows, and steam radiators; artists thrived and imbibed everywhere, painting in the courtyard, turning pottery, or ren-dering charcoal drawings on landings; and the sweet smell of burning marijuana constantly perfumed the air. Since single women occupied most of the apartments, and since the rent was cheap, Berthea Street was a young man's working-your-way-up-in-the-world paradise.

Due to proximity, I first met Vanessa, Alex, and Ted. Vanessa re-sided right below me on the ground floor. She was a graduate student at Rice University, studying classical music and intent on practicing the piano day and night. Her eyes were as blue as topaz, and she had blonde hair, a supple figure, and gave off a down-to-earth but knowing vibe.

Alex described herself as the black sheep of a prominent Houston family, although she taught at a public elementary school and had been cited as the Houston Independent School District's teacher of the year. She was a long-haired brunette with coffee-colored eyes and a striking figure. She had named her pet dachshund Harley, and giving a further nod to the biker lifestyle, she often wore black leather and denim. She loved to peel out of the parking lot at all hours in her Mazda RX-7, like a racecar driver. She was always up for any immediate thrill or dare, so I felt lucky that her apartment was next to mine.

Ted lived next door to Vanessa and perpetually attempted to cultivate an air of refinement, leaving his apartment door open so his classical music—Mozart, Brahms, or Beethoven—crescendoed through the air. The Berthea Street apartments were already too loud; you could hear the murmur of conversations or the vigor of sex through the floors and walls, and voices constantly echoed through the hallways. Ted's loud music annoyed me. Upon first entering his apartment, I was struck by how distinctly feminine the yellow walls looked, as pale as butter, while the end tables were neatly decorated with potted orchids and ferns. Hemingway and Faulkner novels filled the bookshelves, but I never saw Ted reading. The centerpiece of his living room was a chessboard with carved ivory pieces waiting primly on a mahogany coffee table; when we'd first met, Ted asked immediately, "Will you accept my challenge to a game?"

He was stocky with broad shoulders; meaty arms; an imposing bulging stomach; short, blonde, curly hair; and his left eye was covered by an eye patch. The eye, he explained, was afflicted with cancer, so he was being treated with radiation. He always wore brightly colored polo shirts, long shorts, and leather sandals. He claimed to have received a business degree, and added that he was taking additional courses at the University of St. Thomas.

My first impulse was to fend Ted off because he was boring and without enough acumen to justify his quasi-elitism. Vanessa and Alex were more polite and gracious, indulging his requests to visit. When they told me he liked to serve merlot or cabernet, I laughed at the transparent pretentiousness of his *modus operandi*. Would he also offer Swedish massages? Speak of a past career as a French chef? Alex began to ignore him, seeing through his seductive facade, but Vanessa found refusal more difficult due to living next door.

As if fate was determined to prevent my being alone, Alex started inviting me to drink or get high in her apartment every Friday. Afterward, we would go out and try to find the best happy hours. Men constantly sent Alex drinks from across the floor or from distant tables, struck by her vivaciousness and good looks. Complimentary drinks were also sent my way—if Alex were single, her admirers wanted to demonstrate a notable largesse by being polite and hospitable since I appeared to be, at the very least, her friend, but if we were a couple, they wanted to congratulate me. In spite of endless advances, Alex told me that she had never picked up anyone at a bar.

One Friday night, though, a contingent of Middle Easterners asked if we wanted to continue partying with them elsewhere. Alex was amenable, so to stay with her, I consented. As the men headed out and we followed in her car, she told me there would probably be cocaine. I nodded and immediately regretted going. Soon we entered a condominium near the M.D. Anderson Cancer Center. Within seconds, Alex disappeared into the bathroom with three of the men, while I sat drinking at a kitchen table with two others.

When Alex didn't emerge after a while, I rose from my chair. "You shouldn't go in," one of the men seated across from me said. I ignored him. Just as I did when running a race, I drew upon mental toughness and strode down the hallway. Shoving open the bathroom door, I discovered Alex leaning back against the edge of a vanity with glazed eyes, higher than I had ever seen her. One of the three men was attempting to remove her blouse. "We're leaving now," I said, my voice brazen, my stern eyes warning the three men away.

They were recent immigrants, Asian-Americans like I was, but I sensed from the doubt in their exchanged stares that they feared—most likely because of how forcefully I spoke—what I might do if they threatened me. So they glared but didn't interfere as I led Alex away. The thought occurred to me later that I had exhibited Hemingwayesque grace under pressure, having appeared calm on the outside while saving Alex from certain sexual assault. I drove off with her in her RX-7, making our way back to Berthea Street where I tucked her securely into her own bed. The next morning she knocked on my apartment door, stopping by for coffee. "What happened last night?" she asked. "Did you have a good time?"

That same fall, Alex told me about the time she was walking Harley and a married couple that owned an upscale brick house a few blocks away had warned her that for several weeks, cats had gone missing throughout the neighborhood.

"How many cats?" I asked.

"They said over a dozen."

"That's creepy. Don't walk Harley alone anymore late at night," I said.

Soon fear enshrouded the neighborhood like an atomic mushroom cloud, because not only were cats disappearing, but some began to turn up dismembered in plastic trash bags left on the front steps of their owners' houses. For several weeks, no leads were reported. Then one morning Alex pounded on my apartment door. Agony constricted her voice as she asked me to call Vanessa, and then Alex told both of us, "You won't believe this. A guy called the couple that told me about the missing cats, and he said to them, 'You didn't take good care of your cat, and you should take better care of your daughter.' Since the husband works for the District Attorney's office, they have Caller ID. He told me that Ted was the one who called them. *Ted who lives right here!*"

The news that Ted was the cat killer spread through Berthea Street faster than a virus, since the threatened couple had talked with everyone in the neighborhood. The couple had also filed an order of protection which mandated that Ted remain several hundred yards away from their house. By early afternoon, like a grassroots collective, all of the Berthea Street tenants demanded to the property manager that Ted be evicted. To everyone's relief, he was sent packing by dinnertime. His last name was Lacko—from that day on, he became known as Lacko the Whacko. Vanessa felt sickened by the realization that she could have easily wound up as his first human victim, but how could anyone have known? Who could have anticipated having a next-door neighbor who was a serial animal murderer on the verge of broadening his range to include humans?

While Ted was hastily moving out of his apartment, he vociferously insisted to several people in the parking lot that he was moving to receive proper medical treatment for his eye, that it wasn't fair to evict him—the radiation had been affecting his brain. We breathed easier as soon as he was gone, but we remained diligent about making sure that our doors were always locked.

Nevertheless, after only a week, my phone rang one night—Vanessa sounded terrified as she begged me to hurry downstairs. "Please, help me," she whispered. "Ted is outside my window."

As I stepped into Vanessa's apartment, she told me in disbelief, "He's asking if I'll go to the movies with him."

I felt very afraid and somewhat like Truman Capote, knowing I would soon be standing face to face with a killer, directly confronting someone monstrous.

Being a child of the '60s, imagining how I'd respond if physically threatened invariably led me to contemplate the conviction expressed by Dr. Martin Luther King, Jr. in his *1964 Nobel Peace Prize Lecture*: "Nonviolence is a powerful and just weapon which cuts without wounding and ennobles the man who wields it."

Likewise, the civil rights activist, James Lawson, wrote in his 1960 *Student Nonviolent Coordinating Committee Statement of Purpose*: "Nonviolence as it grows from Judaic-Christian traditions seeks a social order of justice permeated by love...Such love goes to the extreme; it remains loving and forgiving even in the midst of hostility."

I also considered the position of Malcolm X expressed in his *Message to the Grass Roots*: "Be peaceful, be courteous, obey the law, respect everyone, but if someone puts his hand on you, send him to the cemetery."

So I could have retreated with Vanessa, adhering to a nonviolent stance by fleeing upstairs with her and calling the police. But Ted had profoundly frightened her. Seeing him there, I grew angry. The window had bars on the outside, but because the lower transom and pane of glass had been raised, only the bars and a screen separated us. Ted stood in the shadows just beyond the range of an overhead spotlight, lurking like a stalker. He frowned when he saw me, and because I was focused on protecting Vanessa, I didn't stop to think that he might be carrying a weapon. Drawing closer, I stared straight into his eyes; he looked indignant, as if I had no right to intrude upon his private discussion with Vanessa. My chest tightened, my heart rate spiked, and anger roiled through my veins. I sensed—just like on that downtown basketball court—that if I displayed any sign of fear or weakness it would be immediately perceived. Ted would then feel entitled to continue imposing upon Vanessa, the illusion persisting in his mind that he was superior, stronger, and more cunning than I. I wasn't about to let him establish any sort of dominance.

Before he could say a word, I spoke in an authoritative, low voice, "Ted, you're not fooling anyone. We all know why you were evicted, and I'm not some little kid you can threaten over the phone. Vanessa won't be going to the movies with you, either. You have to leave now, or I'll call the police."

Ted began mumbling, but I cut him off. "You don't scare me, and I don't want to hear any excuses."

As he opened his mouth, I interrupted him again. "Ted, I don't want to hear another God-damned word."

Ted's assertive expression crumpled, and he squeezed his eyes shut. His head bobbed as if he were contemplating a threat or some sort of retaliation, but before he could say a word, I raised my voice and shouted: "I told you, there's nothing here for you! Walk away, now!"

My aggressiveness determined the outcome. Ted stepped backwards, slipping further into the shadows. As he turned and padded away stealthily, I noticed how agile he was for his size; there was an ursine quality, a concealed strength about him; I felt as though I were watching danger incarnate.

"I'm not staying here tonight," Vanessa said. She slammed the window shut, and I nodded my agreement.

She didn't stay with Alex or me, and within a few weeks she was dating a trumpet player. By the end of that summer, they had moved into a house together. Alex helped me to find a quieter apartment for my writing on nearby Hawthorne Street, and we stayed close for a while, still drinking and going to happy hours together, but then she moved, and unfortunately we lost touch. Years later, I heard she was married and embracing motherhood.

By then, I couldn't help believing that if I were ever challenged, the central guiding principle behind my identity should be aggression; that is, I should respond to any threat fiercely, conveying bravado with a muscular intensity. Since I hadn't intentionally ever sought out conflict, I thought this mindset was appropriate, and that it would require no apologies. Hadn't I already preserved my own sense of self and integrity and protected those close to me? Hadn't I always kept myself from being a victim and avoiding physical harm? I felt psychologically self-determined, rationalizing my own strong-willed, indestructible ethos.

~

But now I was forty-seven, locking eyes at Wal-Mart with a far younger man, a man who was motivated not only by the impending judgment of his own gang, but by the witnesses of a rival gang. The cross-country runners long ago at Central Park had been white, and I'd had confrontations with an African-American, other Asian-Americans, and a certifiably crazy white man, so the race of the Wal-Mart gang members held no real bearing on how I should react. Men versus men—the particular race of any given adversary felt insignificant; it was all the same to me. Glaring at the young gang member, I dismissed him with a scowl, or as the street saying used to go, I looked him off, communicating to him silently that I wouldn't be intimidated. As adrenaline enlivened me, I stepped in front of him and tensed my right arm, prepared to shove him if he put a hand on me, conveying to both gangs that, like some kind of invulnerable middle-aged superman, I wasn't fearful of anyone.

Wariness pervaded my thoughts, though, because of the formula I was carrying for my daughter in a white plastic shopping bag. My infant daughter who had not been in my life before. My wife also waited at home. I had an older adopted daughter now, too. During past confrontations, I had been a bachelor, without people dependent upon my survival. Now I was more aligned with James Lawson's premise, since love prevailed more in my daily life. My right shoulder deterred me, as well, because five months earlier I had undergone surgery for a torn labrum and bone spurs. The doctor's consultation still repeated itself frequently in my brain: "You have the shoulder of someone ten years older. What have you been doing?" I had smiled, telling him that I'd probably cast over a million casts during a lifetime of fishing.

My infant daughter, my wife, my adopted daughter, a lifetime. Ten years older. I wasn't young anymore; I was in my late forties. And the risk that aggression always involves restrained me, kept me from talking

harshly to the gang member who was now trembling almost impercep-
tibly, probably wondering because of the scowl from my looking him off
and the fierceness in my eyes whether he really wanted to prove himself
against an older man, as if the fight looming outside with a rival gang
wasn't enough.

Still, both of us walked toward the exit; a few more steps, and I
would be out in the parking lot with him and over two dozen other
defiant gang members. Fear shone in the eyes of the young gang member while astonishment was rising in the eyes of the other members of
both gangs as they realized what was happening: this was a fight they
hadn't anticipated. But like the character Gurov in Chekhov's classic story "Lady with the Dog", I understood I was no longer the same younger
man. Age *had* caught up with me; I *felt* older; I was older. And so the
masculine sensibility I had believed in didn't make sense anymore and
was no longer viable. But was I capable of responding differently?

Several older African-American and white men were seated at tables, passing the time in a small McDonald's alcove off to the right side.
Some of the men read newspapers, a few drank coffee, and others were
eating hamburgers and fries. What choices do you make to get to be an
old man? Once long ago in Houston, leaving a literary gala, as I walked
beside the poet Adam Zagajewski, many of the well-dressed patrons of
the arts were exiting because the featured speaker, Joyce Carol Oates,
had finished giving her literary talk. The departure had felt like a stam-
pede; men and women alike were clamoring, raising their voices, vying
for attention, holding their tickets high so that the valets would attend
to them promptly and bring their cars around.

"Is there civilization amongst the tuxedos?" I asked Adam.

"No, Allen. Civilization," he wisely replied, "is within yourself."

The earlier defensive moments in my life had been physical, but in
the Wal-Mart, I felt far more cerebral. I didn't like relinquishing my past
masculine identity, but as both gangs swarmed out into the parking lot,
I turned and entered the McDonald's. The young gang member stared

after me, but didn't rebuke me. A girl at the counter took my order for a cheeseburger and fries, and as I sat down and watched with the other older men, as I nurtured an inner idea of civilization, desperate fighting commenced outside. Punches were thrown; bodies soon writhed in pain on the asphalt. I wondered if guns or knives would be pulled. After a few minutes, two Baldwin County sheriffs' cars arrived. The officers quickly broke up the fighting. Part of me still didn't like how I'd been compelled to sit instead of being able to drive home right away, but I felt superior because I'd kept myself out of the fray. Fatherhood, I reflected, was probably good for me.

Since then, I have thought that my behavior that evening was more commensurate with Ralph Abernathy, who spoke at Martin Luther King, Jr.'s 1969 commemorative service. Abernathy posed that "if America is saved, it will be through the black man who can inject new dimensions of non-violence into the veins of our civilization." Indeed, since our nation is no longer thought of as only black and white, Abernathy's words seem applicable not only to African-Americans but to all races. For the time being, I will remain one of the non-violent Americans, unless a more practical sensibility during moments of conflict presents itself. And since my own identity has not remained fixed, my current view of Asian-American masculinity is that it is more like a complex evolving idea, or a life's journey, with the inherent possibility of illuminating moments, extending far beyond emasculatory characterizations.

Silences

n 1920 in California my paternal grandfather, Gee Non Nee, met my grandmother, Lee Sau Young. Although departing for New York he told her, *Don't marry anyone else. I'm headed east to make a fortune, which won't take long. When I'm rich, I'll send for you.*

She later told people she had believed him. Her merchant family was from the city of Canton, while he'd grown up in Toisan on a speck of a farm. She waited for him in San Francisco, and when he sent for her, she rode by train day and night across the country, anticipating that he would be wealthy. Upon her arrival in New York, though, she discovered he was a Chinatown waiter. Too proud to admit to her family that she'd been fooled, too stubborn to retreat back to California, she stayed and married him. How much resentment she harbored because of the concealment of his limited means, or how much she harangued him for the rest of his life to become affluent, has remained part of our family discussions, but my mother has always spoken of my grandmother as a fiery and bitter woman.

Eventually my grandfather became the owner of two restaurants and held interests in others. On many an afternoon, he set out from the family apartment in the Bronx under the pretense of having to look at potential investment properties but rode by subway or taxi down to Chinatown. There, behind curtains or closed doors, he gambled, playing low stakes *mah jong* or *fan tan*, relishing a good time. The betting persisted with a freedom like truancy until my grandmother learned from a Pell Street acquaintance what he was up to, whereupon her scalding voice demanded that the wagering stop. *Otherwise, I'll pack my suitcases and leave with our son. You'll never see him again.* As if a dowager empress had spoken, the gambling ceased immediately. My grandfather didn't say anything, not protesting with one word.

In his prime, my grandfather wore suits; white, long-sleeved, collared shirts; silk ties; gold tie clips; and black dress shoes. He was a tall, lean, congenial man who loved to host a party, far from quiet or inscrutable, so very unstereotypically Chinese. Despite there not being many other Chinese residents in the Bronx, he settled there because of the lower rents. The uncharted territory soon allowed him and his younger brother, my father's Uncle Fred, to open their first restaurant on 167th Street. As success was reaped by working long hours, my grandfather became known to his English-speaking customers as Frank. While opening a second restaurant in the Bronx, he invested in other Chinatown restaurants and practiced a necessary business silence, for in the early nineteen hundreds, fledging Chinese-American companies offered off-the-Wall-Street-market stocks to fellow Chinese. If you desired shares of the future you only needed to provide the requisite cash. The companies ranged from noodle factories to theatres to import-export firms. Some bankrupted, while others survived and flourished. My grandfather participated because during those early years in America, almost no one provided a young Chinese man with the opportunity to learn English, so he needed to do business with other Chinese businessmen. Working from sunrise to midnight rarely left him with any free time to study a new language. He wanted to be a white-collar business executive, but due to his limited ability to speak English, he couldn't traverse the conventional path by attending Harvard Business School or enter the corporate world from any traditional lower rungs. My grandfather never uttered a word to me about his financial practices; I learned of them later from my father.

Likewise, my grandfather never spoke of his entrance into the United States. I didn't know why until one summer. We were traveling to the Canadian side of Niagara Falls, and when my parents stopped their Chevrolet station wagon at the border to display drivers' licenses and copies of our birth certificates, I anticipated that we would be routinely granted permission to enter the country. But when my grandfather produced his identification papers, the border patrolman directed us to the curb.

My grandfather sat beside me in the backseat, not speaking, his hands resting squarely on his lap, his body rigid, eyes directed forward, face proud and indomitable; he was like an old lion, his expression unwavering. The patrolman stepped away and remained absent for several minutes. When he returned my father asked, *What's the delay?*

The patrolman exclaimed, *We haven't ever seen papers like this!*

At that moment I discovered my grandfather had given them his original *Certificate of Identity* from 1908. The laws at that time had required that every Chinese immigrant carry the certificate at all times. The document revealed that he entered the country via Angel Island, alone, at the age of 13, and under the designation of Student. The patrolman said, *I only wanted to show everyone this because of how old and rare it is.* I realized then that my grandfather should have been carrying something more up-to-date, and I have since realized that his waiting with such composure was a traditional Asian mask, a way to save or maintain face. Better to be honorable and project strength, and perhaps escape embarrassment or trouble, than break down and draw unnecessary attention or reveal one's vulnerabilities. He was traditionally masculine, his silence as much a part of him as his blood or his pulse.

Years later my father told me that my grandfather had feared deportation and never admitted the truth about his entrance into the country. My father suspected he was a paper son, probably having purchased someone else's identity. I suspect this was the case, because during his entire lifetime in America, and despite Army service in the nineteen twenties, my grandfather never applied for citizenship. And whenever possible he steered clear of census takers, voter registration drives, and police officers, avoiding public officials at every turn. Sadly, in spite of a great passion for unbridled speed, gleaming wax, shiny chrome, and the glamour and power of automobiles, he couldn't ever bring himself to obtain a driver's license. Despite how any of the Immigration laws that would have affected him had long since been repealed, I think that a small part of him was always afraid, constantly watching his back unless occupied in Chinatown or at one of his restaurants in the Bronx, as convinced that he could be shipped back as he feared the possibilities of being haunted by ghosts or demons. He lived this way, with one eye always open, not speaking of his paper son identity for over sixty-nine years.

My father Eugene's boyhood Chinese name was Gee Yow Jin. Growing up, he worked as a cook in our family's restaurants without wages, as if his contribution were part of his filial duty. He believed that he would be a restaurant cook forever, but when he neared graduation from the Bronx High School of Science, my grandfather told him that he should apply to college, committing to paying the tuition and board in return for all the hours my father had already spent in front of the stoves. A guidance counselor advised my father, *You should study engineering.* Without questioning his opinion, my father became an engineering major in 1954 at the Rensaleer Polytechnic Institute in Troy, three hours north of New York. While he attended classes, my mother Lucy, his high school sweetheart, waited for him in New York, toiling long hours in a Chinatown sweatshop. She sewed, doing piecework, forever callusing her fingers. My father wrote her love letters to bridge the distance, and after completing his bachelor's and master's degrees, he returned to New York prepared to marry her. But in the early stages of the wedding planning, my grandmother announced, *I've been diagnosed with cancer.* The wedding date was advanced several months, and we have speculated that perhaps because my grandmother's own marriage had turned out differently than she had been led to believe, she feared my father might not get married for some reason. After my parents' wedding, my grandmother's cancer diagnosis was never mentioned again, and she lived for another twenty-four years.

My older brother Lawrence was born in Albany in 1960, when my father was upstate seeking engineering work. But he could only find employment with a private firm in Astoria, in the borough of Queens, where I was born in 1962. My grandfather spoke proudly of having two grandsons—we were his little men—and he became effusive with appreciation whenever my father brought us into the restaurants. Drumsticks or even lobster claws were thrust into our hands, and my grandfather would pick us up and shoulder us back to the kitchens to show off to the waiters and cooks. Since the family was together in New York City, time hurried by and happiness abounded, but when I was five, my father received an offer to work as a bridge designer for the New York State Department of Transportation in Albany. The salary, benefits, and potential for advancement were too good to refuse, so within a month, a blue Allied Van Lines truck delivered our belongings north. As we made the journey in our car, I did not know the trip would become one that I would repeat over the following weeks and months, or that eventually I would be able to recite the name of every exit along the Thomas E. Dewey Thruway, because my father, forever a loyal son, would drive us back and forth from Albany to New York for countless family visits.

We were the second family to buy a house toward the end of Van Wie Terrace in the suburb of Guilderland. The first family was white like all the rest would be, and even though we'd arrived early on, some would still claim we didn't belong. My older brother and I became the only Asian minorities at an otherwise all-white school; being a child prodigy who already played piano sonatas, the world of music sheltered my brother. On one of my first days at recess, however, I found myself surrounded; someone demanded, as if I were a sideshow amusement, *Speak Chinese!* When I didn't say a word, shoving and slurs began, followed by fists striking at my head. I had a bloody lip, and my knees were skinned when I fell to the ground. My palms stung from sharp, gray, embedded stones. I did not cry out, my silence a show of strength and defiance. Like a warrior, I pulled myself up and slugged two of the bullies, sending them running. I rode the bus home, trudged into our house, and stormed past my mother. She met my upset face with tender eyes that were afraid for me, but since I remained silent, she didn't know what to say. When my father sought me out later and coaxed me to reveal what had happened, he said, *It's not fair. They were wrong.* But he couldn't offer any retaliatory measures or any reasons for my being harmed; city life in a more racially harmonious Chinese and Jewish Bronx neighborhood and the sedateness of a top-notch engineering university hadn't prepared him for such trials.

During the subsequent weeks and months, I viewed my father as invisible, since he couldn't help me deal with bullying. We seemed to have nothing in common. I wished for something—anything—to affirm we were alike, but as I became interested in competing in contact sports, he couldn't teach me how to throw a football, shoot a basketball, pitch a baseball, or swing a bat. He wasn't familiar with the world of rugged athletics. So one sports season after another, I struggled to coach myself or improve through the sheer repetition of endless practicing alone. For the most part, my efforts were doomed. My frustration over feeling perpetually inadequate or unknowing led to continual eruptions; I swung my fists at doors or walls, and when my father ordered me to tell him what was wrong, I raged in silence, knowing he couldn't help. Since I offered no explanation, he accused me of being too short tempered and too sensitive, which led to my defying him by extending the silence, not speaking to him about anything. The gap between us widened. If I did ask for his opinion, he only said, withholding any real opinions, *Make what you think is the best decision.* This became the pattern of our limited conversation until I reached eighteen. For all purposes, like a master eschewing a petulant disciple, my father had raised me in silence. I felt isolated, like I lived in another dimension or an eternally gloomy world.

At first my grandfather had approved of our move to Albany, asserting that Chinatown, the Bronx, and all of New York City didn't offer enough opportunities. *America,* he told us, *is too big, too rich to know just one part.* But then he didn't like the distance separating our family, so my father began driving us on weekends—twice if not three times a month—from Albany to New York and back. My mother soon gave birth to a third son, Brian, causing my grandfather to object to the distance even more. During one weekend visit, he and I sat alone at the back corner table at one of his restaurants. Receipts and bills covered the table, and since the spot served as a good vantage point, he poured some tea and scanned the long rectangular dining room filled with round tables and gold booths. Once he felt reassured that the waiters were properly serving all the customers, he lit a Pall Mall cigarette and asked, *Gay ho ma?* How are you?

Okay, I said in English.

He asked, *How's school?*

I was in junior high by then and told him, lying, *It's all right.* This elicited a frown, because I wasn't speaking any Chinese. He didn't verbally chastise me, reserving any arguments about how I spoke for my parents. In New York, Chinese kids often attended American schools by day and Chinese schools at night to maintain their native dialects, but no school in Albany offered Cantonese, so my grandfather believed my parents should have been teaching me our family dialect at home.

He gazed at me with a mixture of regret and understanding and asked, *Do you know what your Chinese name means?* I had never considered that there might be a significant meaning for my Chinese name, *Gee Wing Fook* (the k silent). My grandfather nudged aside some of the bills and receipts on the table and dug out a small pad of paper. On an empty page in black ink, he scrawled out the three Chinese characters for my name and said, *The first part, Gee, means honor. The second part, Wing, means forever. The third part*—he smiled—*means wealth.*

As an adult I would realize that my name matched the rationale of an immigrant, one whose grandson would search with honor forever and find wealth, but at that moment in the restaurant, I didn't comprehend much of the meaning or see how my name was related to my older brother's, *Gee Wing Horn*, or my younger brother's, *Gee Wing Jiu*. I was simply glad to have learned a little more about my name. Soon a waiter brought us *chow fun*, rice noodles, and we started eating. I felt at ease and safe there in my grandfather's restaurant; each trip to the city seemed to emphasize how wrong the decision to move to Albany had been. My being Chinese had never posed problems in New York. I frequently dreamed of moving back someday, or living with my grandparents instead, but such a return never occurred. Likewise, my grandfather never brought up the subject of my name again.

In 1977 at eighty-two, my grandfather was hospitalized because of diabetes and other complications furthered by decades of smoking Pall Malls. The doctors said that the cigarettes had ravaged his body, destroying his recuperative powers. My grandmother summoned us repeatedly to New York, so we drove back and forth each week, leaving on Thursday nights or Friday mornings. During our visits to the hospital, when my grandfather asked how I was or how business fared at his restaurants, I said I was managing just fine or that the dining rooms appeared busy. Once he requested that I smuggle in some Chinese food, so I brought him slices of roast duck and Chinese broccoli. On another morning he greeted me with the firmest of handshakes but declared our visit would have to be brief because the doctors were running some tests. He asked about my high school and how things were in Albany. Soon an orderly arrived, so my grandfather instructed me to look up at his window from the street below after I reached the ground floor and walked out. Upon leaving his room, I rode the elevator down and walked outside. I stood on the sidewalk like a rock in the middle of a river's currents as pedestrians swarmed around me. I strained my neck, gazing up at my grandfather's window until he materialized; he stood in the glass for a moment and waved—on his feet, strong, authoritative, the image he'd always wanted to exude—and once I waved back, he vanished. That was the last time I saw him alive, but I had yet to learn about his other considerable acts of silence.

Through the Holt Adoption Agency, my parents adopted a three-year-old girl in 1978, naming her Catherine. They explained to my brothers and me that they'd always wanted a daughter and weren't leaving anything to chance. I hadn't known about the adoption application, which my parents had filed in 1975. We met our new sister at LaGuardia Airport, the flight originating from Seoul, Korea. An interpreter said to my sister in Korean, *This is your father, mother, and three brothers*, and then left us without another word. We stopped at my Uncle John's and Aunt Myrna's place in Douglaston, Long Island before the long drive back to Albany. When my father remarked that my grandfather had known and approved of the adoption of a girl, I felt surprised yet again by another example of his forward thinking.

By the time I departed for the University of New Hampshire in 1980, I began to see more clearly what type of man my father actually was. He was more visionary than I had realized—the education I'd received from the better suburban schools in Albany allowed me to select from several strong colleges. In typical noncommittal fashion, he told me to go to whatever university I judged to be best and to choose whatever major I wanted, but he added that unlike the majors chosen by Chinese-Americans who felt pressured to conform, my major could be different than engineering, music, or mathematics. Still, before I left, he didn't initiate any kind of meaningful conversation about the displacement of my youth, as if there had never been any sort of rift between us, as if my difficult years had never occurred. But I didn't fault him for his silence, realizing that he was saving face, or living in the moment, rather than focusing upon any past disagreements.

Within a few short years, my grandmother—her English name was Nellie—required close attention, having become too frail to take care of herself in the Bronx. My father moved her to an apartment in Albany, then to a retirement community in Guilderland called Wellspring House not ten minutes from where we lived. One summer when I was home alone, she telephoned claiming to be sick. When I drove over, though, she stood by the parking lot wearing black bow pumps, a knee-length cobalt blue sheath dress, a matching jacket, and a white circle cloche hat. The most elegant string of white pearls adorned her neck. I ended up taking her shopping at Macy's, then to a nearby Chinese restaurant called The Jade Fountain. *You don't have to tell me you're sick if you want me to visit,* I said to her. She ignored me, her silence communicating to me that her loneliness would never surface as the subject for any conversation. By 1983 her health worsened, and she became very small, looking practically shriveled, refusing to eat. One evening during her last days, my father visited her at the Albany Medical Center. As he sat by her bedside, she leaned toward him and said, *I have to tell you, many years before I met your father, I married another man in California. He was a criminal who did unspeakable things. When I went to the church and asked for help, they convinced me to divorce him. I remain deeply ashamed of the failure of that marriage. But what is worse is something I promised your father that I would never tell you. You were adopted.*

At this point in life, my father was forty-five years old.

My father waited several months until my brothers and sister and I were all at home; he gathered us in the family room with my mother beside him on a couch. After revealing my grandmother's deathbed confession, he remarked to my younger sister, *I guess you're not the only one who's adopted.*

My older brother, now twenty-two and studying music accompaniment at the University of Indiana, asked, *Why was your adoption kept secret?*

My mother told me that they wanted me to feel like I belonged, my father answered, *and that I didn't owe them anything extra. She said that my being their son made them proud and happy enough.*

My younger brother, now fifteen, asked, *Do you know where they adopted you from?*

I have no idea, my father said. *I've checked with our family lawyer. He's sure nothing bad can happen because of all this. My United States citizenship can't be revoked. You don't have to worry about our family name being changed, either.*

Do you want to search for your real parents? my younger sister asked.

No, my father said. *I have the five of you, my job, and our house. My life is full.* He fell silent, but the quiet felt unnatural, so I didn't entirely believe him. Mulling over everything, I compared his announcement with what I had known about his upbringing. Years before, my mother had told me his birthplace was listed as the Yee Farm in New Jersey. The story was that his mother had feared hospitals, so she'd gone to the farm to enlist the services of a Chinese midwife. No one had ever questioned this.

I'd always puzzled about my father being an only child, though, which seemed like an anomaly for a Chinese couple. My grandparents had told him that one child was more than enough to raise in the city. The earliest known photograph of my father was a black and white snapshot: my grandmother cradles him in her arms as my grandfather stands to the right, and my father is bundled up, at least a year old. My grandparents wear thick winter coats. Brick buildings and billboards rise up in the distance, but the city is stark with bare plots of land in the background and empty spaces across the dark skyline. My grandfather's face emanates contentment, but my grandmother's expression is stern. When my father asked his parents about not having any earlier photographs of him, they'd told him that no one at the farm had owned a camera, and photos had cost too much back then. My father would never have accused them of lying; why would he be suspicious? I could easily understand his accepting every word of their explanation.

Before wandering out of the living room, my brothers and sister and I told our father we were glad our family wouldn't change. I wondered, however, what lengths my grandfather had gone to in order to secure the adoption. What had the adoption of a small child entailed in those days? Was it legal? Had my father been born in America? Imagining how my grandparents had probably never sought the opinion of an American doctor or been tested for why they couldn't conceive, I surmised that they might have blamed each other for their infertility during their entire married lives.

When my grandfather's brother Fred died, two of his children—my father's cousins, King and May—telephoned our house in Albany. With wary voices they related the discovery of a folder amongst Fred's possessions. Two weeks later, the cousins drove to Albany, so my father cooked and served a seven-course Chinese meal. As we ate *dan tat,* and custard tarts, and drank tea for dessert, King brought out a thick manila folder and said, *There are records, licenses, permits, leases, bills of sale, and purchase orders, but I also found these.* On the table, he placed a black and white photograph, a *Certificate of Identity*, and a single sheet of white paper covered with Chinese characters. In the photograph, a dour-faced young woman was holding a small boy in her right arm. *That's you,* King said to my father, who picked up the photograph and examined it closely. *May and I don't think she's your real mother. She was probably hired to bring you over safely,* King said. My father gasped, having learned his birthplace was not the Yee Farm in New Jersey but in China. When he passed the photograph around and it reached me, I saw that the boy was younger than the earliest photograph I'd seen of my father, but it was unquestionably him. On the white lower border were the words: *BY APPOINTMENT OF THE LATE H.E. SIR ARTHUR KENNEDY K.O.B, A. FONG, HONG KONG,* Emigrant's Photographer. I turned the photograph over and read two names below the heading of *DOLLAR STEAMSHIP LINE: Mrs. Woo Wai Kweng and Msr. Gee Wing Fook.* I couldn't believe it; my father was not really Yow Jin as my grand-parents had called him, but he and I shared the same Chinese name. His age was listed as 11 months, and the back of the photograph also includ-ed that he'd been brought over on the *Coolidge*, its sailing date October 20, 1938, its destination San Francisco.

King pointed to the Chinese characters on the sheet of paper and told us that they identified my father's family village in China and his place as second in a line of several brothers. So not only had my grand-father concealed my father's adoption, but he'd quietly preserved the tradition of naming brothers sequentially—my father was, like me, a second son.

A few years later, my father and I drove through the old family neigh-borhood in the Bronx. Now mostly Hispanics resided there; we saw no Chinese or Jews walking the streets, and most of the old brick buildings had been leveled, but my grandfather's apartment building still stood.

Do you want to go inside? I said.

I don't think so, my father said.

We rode by my grandfather's first restaurant. It was still a restaurant, except the sign out front read: COMIDAS CHINAS Y LATINAS.

I don't want to see how they've changed the dining room, my father said, and he looked at me with tired eyes that were filled with regret over the loss of his childhood, and then he continued driving.

When I reached my thirties, I learned that my father had become frustrated over not receiving promotions at work; he had been repeatedly passed over in favor of less-qualified whites. I only overheard him speaking of this to my mother on one occasion, but I realized the move to Albany had also exacted costs upon him. In my late thirties, I bravely asked him why he had raised me in silence without ever giving me advice, and his response was, *You were so strong-headed that I knew you'd be fine. I also wanted to raise you to be independent. And I didn't want you to blame me for any bad decisions.* As he had hoped and anticipated, I had become independent, having long since left home; by now I was an English teacher, not conforming to any stereotypical Asian career paths. But my ends didn't seem to justify my father's stark means.

Dad, you could have at least given me your opinion now and then.

Without hesitation, he said, *All right. From now on, I will.*

I am fifty and live in the Deep South now, in Georgia. My father is long retired and recently celebrated his seventy-fifth birthday. An interesting consequence of his retirement was that without the drain of daily office drudgery, he has become much more talkative at home, over the telephone, and via email. We recently had a conversation about our family moving to Albany, during which he asked, *Do you know how many times I was passed over? It started to get to me. They kept promoting less qual-*

ified whites, so I had to ask if there was something wrong with me—even people I had trained were being promoted over me. That was when I knew I had to retire. For a long time after I was gone from the office, they were still trying to reel me in, asking if I would work part-time, but I said no. They can have it.

Bitterness tinged his voice, and I realized that my father and I were similar in ways I hadn't imagined, beyond our shared name and being second sons. He'd been a racial pioneer struggling in hostile territory, like I'd been enduring racism in white classrooms.

He'd also lost the security of being amongst so many other Asians in New York City and Chinatown. Still, he'd remained devoted to providing for his family, in spite of his career discouragement. I admired how for four decades he'd never complained to us about the limitations of his job, never taking any frustration out on my mother, my brothers and sister, and me. Indeed, he'd always maintained a placid and calm disposition, as peaceful as the surface of a windless lake, which was yet another longstanding silence. So as I look back over the years, reaching adulthood seems to mean, in my family, that by then, one should understand not only the inadequacy of silence, but also appreciate the dignity of it.

And further considering how silence has pervaded our family, I know it is not simply something mysterious, shameful, confounding, and divisive; nor is silence something to be resented. It is a behavior that will forever be in the air, seeming as natural as the wind or the sun. For although I might wish otherwise, not only is silence a deeply ingrained part of our history, but I sense it's deep in our bones, as if it's a part of our destiny, and so in its many forms, it will most likely continue.

Point Guard

Point

I am a nervous boy, a foundling, a pure neophyte, learning how to hold a basketball as my sixth grade physical education teacher, Joe Torres teaches our class how to correctly take a jump shot. Most of us are too small to launch the ball accurately; we seem outmatched, rarely reaching the backboard square. Though sports seem as intimidating as summiting Mount Everest, they appear to be one way for me to assimilate, to feel a sense of belonging, because the year is 1974 and nearly my entire suburban junior high school is white. The melting pot theory is common currency; every immigrant might, because of America's greatness, somehow be able to fit in by learning how to be Caucasian, regardless of the attributes of our own cultures.

Guard

"You don't get respect for being an Asian-American basketball player in the U.S." said Lin. As Northern California's Division II player of the year who led Palo Alto to a Division II State Championship, he expected some Division I scholarship offers but got none. On the road he get taunts like, Go back to China!" and "Open your eyes!"[1]

Interior Meta-Monologue #1:

In 2012, Jeremy Lin averaged 23.9 points and 9.2 assists during his first 11 games as the starting point guard for the NY Knicks. He also shot over fifty percent. Since he was the first Asian-American to rise to prominence in the NBA fans went wild. The term Linsanity quickly grabbed hold. Can my own personal basketball memoirs say enough about Lin? Probably not. But Guy Debord's Spectacle of Society tells us, the

---

[1] Jeff. "Jeremy Lin and the Challenges Facing Asian American Athletes" *8Asians.com*, Dec. 16, 2008.

The more enlightened idea of universal tolerance and cross appreciation waits a decade in the future. As I hold the full-sized basketball it almost overwhelms my hands, but my coordination is better than most; shooting with my legs and body, I send the ball on a high arc. It bounces off the top of the backboard square, gravity taking over so the ball drops downward and falls cleanly through the net. Joe Torres glances over, somewhat startled, but then concentrates and appears to be making a mental note, his wizened expression saying, *You bear watching.*

Yes, I want to fit in, falsely believing that if I can play sports like anyone I will be like any other students, and whites will notice or taunt me less, so when our next door neighbor, Harold Williams, asks if I want to shoot baskets with him and his son, Kevin, because they have a new basketball hoop, I assent and run over to their driveway. Harold is gangly, six-foot five, a former high school player. When he challenges his son and me to one-on-two games his height becomes pandemic: he can't be

spectacle presents itself simultaneously as all of society, as part of society, and as instrument of unification.[2] To me, Linsanity should be viewed as a spectacle of the highest magnitude.

At some point, Jeremy Lin ceased being a basketball player and morphed into something closer to a national phenomenon. He's Linsanity... But he's also something far more meaningful and potentially historic. He's the dream-carrier for masses of Asian-Americans.[3] But as a reedy Asian-American (from Harvard, no less) Lin simply didn't fit anyone's image of an NBA guard.[4]

With Lin's rise, there has been a feeling, a swelling collective feeling, that we Asians are no different from the other people we see on national TV, almost exclusively white and black. That we are Jeremy Lin, able to play as well as they in "their" arena, the ability of Jeremy Lin pointing to us all.[5]

Because long-time superstars like Kobe Bryant earn upwards of $25 million a year, "the average annual NBA salary is more than $5 million.

2 Guy Debord, *Society of the Spectacle*. **Black & Red.** **Detroit, 1983. Section**

3 Dave Zirn. "Jeremy Lin Inspires a Nation." *The Nation*, March 19, 2012.

4 James Surowicki. "Linjustice." *The New Yorker*, March 5, 2012.

5 Matthew Salesses. "Different Racisms: On Jeremy Lin and How the Rules of Racism are Different for Asian-Americans." *The Rumpus*, March 2012.

defeated, looming over us like a harbinger of cold reality. If Kevin and I drive to the basket too aggressively, Harold swats down our shots; if we try to score standing too close to Harold, he blocks the ball. To keep the games going, sometimes he relents and gives us the gift of a score, or if he lapses intentionally we sense it, so no win for us is a real victory. But all spring my fundamental skills of dribbling and passing and shooting are being developed, and racial harmony thrives within that small rectangular space. We enjoy the exercise; we laugh at our own mistakes. Yet since I am five-foot six and Harold and Kevin are both so much taller than me, through no fault of their own, I am already conscious of my fitting into the American mindset that Asians are naturally shorter and therefore physically inferior, aside from how much determination I bring to the court.

My father, perhaps wanting me to have a "normal" childhood, or simply being a responsible parent keeping up with my activities, observes how much I'm playing basketball next door. Out of generosity or in the spir-

Indeed, Lin's salary, at $800,000, is the NBA's "minimum wage" for a second-season player.[6]

The team had won again seven straight wins in a row... He was link-bait, like bait; there were encomiums and paeans, and stats, followed by dismissals which were followed by more games more scoring, more YouTube videos videos, followed by more praise, more doubters. Memes. People were fighting pro-Lin/con- like they were Democrats and Republicans and this was Bush vs. Gore. There was a FOX Sports commentator Tweet scandal followed by a demand for an apology and then the apology... you can see there are two games Lin is playing and winning—one is basketball, the other is the game the American media complex plays in making you think X about Asians.[7]

Jason Whitlock's inner struggling comedian made a desperate play for attention, and it resulted in Whitlock falling flat on his face. As Jeremy Lin shredded the Los Angeles Lakers for 38 points, Whitlock (FOX News) typed this tweet:

Jason Whitlock ≫ Follow ▲▾

Some lucky lady in NYC is gonna feel a couple inches of pain tonight.

6 Greg Mankiw. "Rogoff reflects on Jeremy Lin." *Greg Mankiw's Blog.* March 3, 2012.

7 Alexander Chee. "The Jeremy Lin Economy." *The Classical.* February 16, 2012. pp. 1-4. (I admire Chee's spirited and intelligent writing on Lin).

it of assimilation, he asks if I want a backboard and goal of my own. So I watch that same week, grateful, with a twelve-year-old's wonder, as a plumbing company truck delivers the thickest steel pipe over half a foot in diameter. A deep hole is dug, and the pipe is reinforced with a construction grade cement footing. To this day, the pole and backboard stand. I begin to use the court daily, practicing right and left hand layups, long bank shots, dribbling left, right, spinning, or imitating the Knicks' Walt "Clyde" Frazier and Earl "The Pearl" Monroe—jumping, launching my body like I aspire to flight, devoting hours to the game that leave my arms, legs, wrists and hands sore, my lungs gasping as my head lowers and my hands sink to my knees. And when I score or sink basket after basket at the painted white foul line there is an order to the world, a feeling that—at least for a few minutes—I have some sort of control. It is a very peaceful space; racism and bullying do not exist, the court like a church, a retreat from taunts or fights; it is a world of my own. Since my older brother soars as a music prodigy,

Needless to say, this didn't go over so well.[8]

Interior Meta-Monologue #2:

The "dream-carrier" line of thinking and that a pro-basketball player would be the one to make an entire race feel "no different"are troubling quotes; they're disturbing. They assume that you allow other races to tell you you're inferior, to define who you are, and while self-hatred is a very real psychological condition in this country, it doesn't speak for all of Asian-America. Many of my Asian friends in Houston who I watched Yao Ming play for the Rockets with didn't need Jeremy Lin to make them feel better about themselves. We were already proud of being Asian.

If one needs Jeremy Lin to feel better about being Asian, then here's a very real question. Why not reject any kind of psychological aspects of culture that are, ultimately, furthering white supremacy? Why heed any kind of message that starts with the assumption that Asians are less than? Isn't this the core belief of the Klu Klux Klan? Or Neo-Nazi skinheads? I mean, really?

And about Jason Whitlock: where are we when a paid professional,

8 Richard Langford. "Jason Whitlock Shows True Colors on Twitter with Lame Jeremy Lin Tweet." *Bleacher Report.* Feb. 14, 2012.

his playing notes and scales and learning new pieces on the piano day in day out constantly floods our house with classical music, so I am yet more pleased to be dribbling away, wearing out one pair sneakers after another on the pavement. During the stifling heat of summer, I practice until my head whirls from dizziness, and when winter arrives I shovel off the driveway by hand and play on, a true devotee, despite freezing cold or falling snow.

My parents send me the next year to Siena College's overnight summer basketball camp where I am, of course, the only Asian-American attendee. Siena is a small private Catholic school coached by Bill Kirsch and will eventually make the NCAA tournament. They are building their program by scouring the local streets for talent, and my coach for the week, Walt Bellamy, notes my hustle and realizes the extent of my superior coordination, so when putting me through drills he pays extra attention and speaks and looks at me with a different level of urgency. I dribble the ball, the rock, behind my back from

who is a person of color, expresses himself by insulting a fellow person of color, perpetuating the worst of emasculating stereotypes?

The Jeremy Lin Word Generator.

Lin + [insert here]= [Linsert here].[9]

10. Lin It to Win It! **9.** The Lin Crowd **8.** Linsider **7.** Lint Condition **6.** Ooh, Ling (Ewing) **5.** Linscrafters **4.** Linnin **3.** Lin Time **2.** Lin Man **1.** Lin[10]

Jeremy, I want You LINside me.[11]

Why is there so much hype, though? It has to die out at some point. Oh, you know how white people are. We're fairly certain that black people are physically gifted and Asian people are mentally gifted, and it's, like, so wild when those conceptions are shattered by a charming, capable young man who happens to be both![12]

Jimmy Zheng, in Chinatown on Wednesday evening, just wanted to see Lin on television. No one—in Chinatown or elsewhere—knows how long Mr. Lin's magical run will last, or if anything like it, for Asian-Americans, will ever be seen again.[13]

9 "The Jeremy Lin Word Generator." *Linwords.com.*

10 Anthony Crave. "Jeremy Lin Sayings." *Askmen. com.*

11 Matt Stopera. "The Best Jeremy Lin Sign Yet." *Buzzfeed.com.* Feb. 25, 2012.

12 Explainer. "The Non Sports Fan's Guide to Jeremy Lin." *The Gawker.*

13 Ken Belson. "Chinatown Can Cheer, But Can't Watch, Rise of an Adopted Star." *New York Times.* Feb. 15, 2012.

right to left or left to right, and between my legs, and we start to work on a crossover dribble. Walt also teaches me the angles of the reversal and how to use the rim to protect my shot when I drive to the basket. We throw bounce passes, behind the back passes, wraparound and no-look passes, diverting the defender's eyes with a glance in one direction while sending the basketball elsewhere. I remember Joe Torres' jump shot lesson as I actually develop a little fade away jump shot from within the foul line. Coach Kirsch gives all two-hundred attendees a lecture about how to handle a basketball with your fingertips: *You love the basketball. So you need to hold it the same way you want to touch your girlfriend.* At this point, I'm only in the seventh grade so his lecture seems like an indecipherable language, but three years later when I have my first girlfriend, I remember what he says.

At the basketball camp I become known for leaping because my calves are muscular—a few years later when my vertical leap is measured, it will be thirty-six inches—and when Walt

Interior Meta-Monologue #3:

Jeremy Lin, or the spectacle of linsanity, will last as long as the public fuels it, by watching Lin on television, buying basketball tickets, t-shirts, jerseys, posters, and there are even action-figures.. Debord tells us that not only is the spectacle a collection of images, "but a social relation among people, mediated by images."[14] All of the punning off Lin's name is yet another sign to me of how America has to treat Lin as exotic—Me Love You Lin Time—because the media can't normalize an Asian-American male's masculinity or athletic prowess. Debord also says that "the spectacle is the moment when the commodity has attained the total occupation of social life." Of course, athletes are commodities, with precariously short career spans, and what could be more exemplary of "total occupation" than a young woman in Madison Square Garden holding up a "Jeremy, I want you LINside me" sign? What's still wrong with America is that there shouldn't be such surprise and astonishment that anyone of another race, who isn't Caucasian, can be better than average at anything. Far too much of the writing about Jeremy Lin continues to be ignorant and juvenile, when race is the focus. It's not up to Jeremy Lin, or anyone, or all of

14 Debord, Guy. Section 4.

prepares my scrimmage team for the camp's final mini-tournament he asks, *Can you play point guard?* I assent. In the meantime I have made two close friends: Mike Ryan who is Caucasian and Johnnie Ray Wall who is African-American. We are aware of how much our friendship defies racial expectations; our solidarity is such that we become marked. Some try to target us, attempting to take us out with hard fouls in any game we play. We are in different age brackets because Mike is two years older than me (he has already played on the freshmen team for Christian Brothers Academy), while Johnnie is three years older and stands six-feet two (he is a starting guard for metro-power Albany High's varsity team). Coach Kirsch is heavily recruiting Johnnie so we eat a lot of pizza that has been "sent over" to Johnnie's room, and there we talk basketball non-stop or Mike and Johnnie regale me with stories about girls. As the mini-tournament unfolds, each of our teams—in different age brackets—ascends through the pairings, and the three of us cheer each other on until we win

Asian-America, to "show the world" how multi-dimensional we can be. This seems to burden the supposedly downtrodden with solving their own abuse/degradation/dehumanization. It fails to ask where the blame should actually lie for existent misperceptions.

At the same time, he confounds us because we can't create a simple storyline around his identity. Is he an underdog or is he privileged? Does he fit in with the NBA or doesn't he?... the questions we ignore are to what extent we believe that Asian-Americans can't play basketball because they are less "American" and basketball is an "American" sport.[15]

Of course we're far beyond the blatant discrimination that stopped players such Jackie Robinson and Willie Mays from playing in the MLB, but there still is a similar psychological barrier that Lin is currently in the process of dismantling in front of our very eyes, said Dean Adachi, an historian and lecturer of Asian-American Studies.[16]

ESPN issued an apology last night after a racially insensitive headline about New York Knicks star guard Jeremy Lin appeared on their mobile site. The headline,"Chink In The

15 Lakshmi Ramarajan. "Finding the Right Jeremy Lin Storyline." *Harvard Business School Working Knowledge.* March 21, 2012.

16 Jamilah King. "The Subtle Bigotry That Made Jeremy Lin the NBA's Most Surprising Star." *Colorlines.* Feb. 8, 2012.

our respective championships. Our celebration is boldly triumphant, defying our white detractors because we know we represent something better, sensing that it is something revolutionary and uniquely futuristic, although we have no idea what the concept of a post-racial America is. Since I have scored 14 points and made 6 steals in my age-bracket's championship final, Walt reveals that my play at point guard has almost garnered me the M.V.P. award. *Your getting the ball so we could score*, he says, *was the difference.* Still I have my doubts about high school basketball. Can I grow stronger? I am only five-feet seven now, so will I be tall enough? That fall Mike Ryan becomes a body-builder and weightlifter, conceding he's stopped growing and can't leap high enough for a future in basketball. Johnnie throws down a monstrous dunk over a six-ten center that becomes legendary, the stuff of city lore, but in two years upon accepting a full scholarship to Boston University he declares, deflecting any premature hype or NBA speculation, that he knows he'll obtain his marketing de-

Armor," appeared only on mobile browsers, the network said, and only between the hours of 2:30 AM ET and 3:05AM ET.[17]

Bryan Chu: Some might say, why didn't Yao Ming evoke this type of emotion in you? The difference is that Jeremy is one of us. He was born in the U.S. He was that kid who got straight As in school. He was the one that worked at his high school newspaper. He has a bit of an Americanized accent when he speaks Mandarin.[18]

Interior Meta-Monologue #4:

To live too vicariously or look to be Iinspired is slightly unsettling, at the very least, for how much should any human being fetishize a professional basketball player whose career could easily be short-lived due to injury (Lin has already suffered a season-ending injury and surgery for a torn left meniscus in his knee)? ESPN staff writer Anthony Federico's calling Lin a "Chink" with a national network as the delivery system is as blatant as can be; there is no monopoly on racism, especially when it occurs at prominent levels. It's simply about humiliation and destruction. And Chu's comparison of Lin with Yao Ming is short-sighted, at

17 TMZ Sports. "Jeremy Lin—ESPN Apologizes Over Offensive Headline." *www.tmz.com*. February 18, 2012.

18 Adrienne Mong. "Yes, Jeremy Lin is big in China— but China is also very big." *NBC News*. Feb. 16, 2012.

gree. What is clear to me is that my being Asian-American isn't limiting me; I happen to be from a family with a history of a few men who have reached six feet, so race is not a detriment or primary factor, but how much will I grow?

I run cross country during the fall my first year at Guilderland high school, then make the freshmen basketball team that winter and see some playing time. That spring I run the quarter and half mile in track and win some races. But all year my body remains at 5'7". Disappointent aches within me, but fate makes itself clear and irrefutable; I'm not destined to become taller. My speed and size convince me to devote myself to running year round, to take up indoor track during the winter instead of trying out for junior-varsity basketball. The varsity soccer coach has seen me compete at track meets and tries to lure me over to his squad, but I like running more. If I'm not running, like someone mourning for a lost love, I still find myself being drawn back to basketball courts—at parks in downtown Albany or at the Albany YMCA—

best, because it fails to address the culture nationalist aspects of favoring Lin over Ming. We can only root more for someone Asian who is "one of us?" I enjoyed watching Yao Ming play as much as I've enjoyed watching Jeremy Lin play. We are simply limited, provincial Asian-Americans if we can't appreciate the athletic endeavors of any Asian player who is competing in the NBA.

Many fans donned No. 17 jerseys and T-shirts, some of them waving posters saying 'Lincredible" and "Bal-lin." Since Lin's Feb. 4 breakout game, sales at online Knicks-linked stores—which carry about 50 Lin-related items—have surged forty fold, while sales at the arena are up 70%, according to management, with Lin-related gear accounting for about half of online sales and about a third of in-arena sales...The Knicks held a 39% peak market share of the $3 billion NBA merchandise market in the week ending Feb. 25, when Lin merchandise reached stores nationwide.[19]

According to the @nikestore account, the Nike Zoom Hyperdunk 2011 Low Jeremy Lin "Away" PE will be releasing online at the Nike Store on May 26th. Will you be picking these up this weekend?[20]

---

[19] Andria Chang. "Jeremy Lin's Star Not Fading Off Court." *Sportswatch*. March 20, 2012.

[20] Jacques Slade. "Zoom Hyperdunk 2011 Lower Jeremy Lin 'Away' PE." *Knicksonfire.com*. May 26, 2012.

and a past rival named Rich Tocci who I played against as a freshman now often calls. We meet up to play pickup games because he's a deadly shooting guard and likes how I know when and where to pass him the ball. For the next three years, during the summer months, we dominate at the city playground court adjacent to the Oswald D. Heck Psychiatric Center, or during winter and spring breaks we win and hold the full court at the Y. As much as I love the game, my body is taking a beating; since my success depends more now upon speed, I absorb endless hard fouls driving to the basket. This is bearable on the playground or at the Y., but one low bridge—having my knees cut out from under me—or being struck or clotheslined with a forearm by a larger player in high school or college could hobble or injure me for life. Still during those three years, I learn this:

When you feel that you can affect or dictate the flow of the game by determining the pace— by scoring on your own and creating opportunities for teammates, or by shutting down an opponent or outplaying him or

Volvo has officially signed Jeremy Lin to a global endorsement deal, and the New York Knicks point guard will serve as the new Volvo brand ambassador worldwide...Volvo says the athlete's character, intelligence and perseverance all dovetail with the brand's ethos...According to Automotive News, Volvo aims to increase the company's global sales to 800,000 units by 2020, with much of that increase aimed at the Chinese market. Last year, the company sold around 47,000 vehicles in China.[21]

Interior Meta-Monologue #5:

Can prose and quotes alternating throughout an essay from right to left make up for not playing point guard any longer? Or is literary creativity equal or superior to the joy of being physically conditioned and possessing athletic skill?

...the U.S. Patent and Trademark office has rejected the remaining applicants for the Linsanity trademark. Lin is the only candidate remaining, says his lawyer, Pamela Diese. The name 'Linsanity' appeared on everything from T-shirts to medical marijuana dispensers selling Linsanity pot.[22]

---

[21] Zach Bowman. "Volvo Announces Jeremy Lin Endorsement Contract." *Autoblog.com*. March 20, 2012.

[22] Staff Report. *Sporting News*.

her—or when you are dominant because of your vision, dribbling, and passing or shooting skills, and when you want the ball and everyone looks to you and wants to get you the ball so that you are the locus of play, like a conductor or floor general, or when you are the man, the woman or the one whose play determines whether your team wins or loses in "clutch" moments, only then do you know what it is to be a "true" point guard. Having experienced this, I have known for years that Asian-Americans are more than capable of playing the position, so it's been inevitable that more of us would appear on the court.[23]

My last significant basketball moment is during my freshman year at the University of New Hampshire when I'm playing pickup ball in the main gymnasium. Some guys wearing UNH Basketball t-shirts stride out; I know they play for the university. The point guard who matches up against me is African-American—I later discern he's their starting guard—but the first time I bring the ball up, I slash by him

Interior Meta-Monologue #6:

With free agency, the Knicks faced resigning Lin or matching an offer from the Houston Rockets for $25 million over 3 years. Debord observes that "The spectacle subjugates living men to itself to the extent that the economy has totally subjugated them."[24] Knick fans howled for management to retain Lin. MSG's stock fell 2.2% when news spread that the Knicks might not keep him. Since the spectacle is really only the mask of the commodity, it's dangerous to become attached, to expect fan loyalty to matter, because the NBA is ultimately about business analysts running numbers. Of course, boys who worship basketball and practice for endless hours in their driveways for the pure love of the game have no knowledge of this, nor should they.

...Lin alone may contribute 10% to the Knicks bottom line. That would amount to only 1% of MSG's total revenue, or about $12 million. Lin was also a boon to merchandising, food and beverage sales, but those segments represent a tiny portion of MSG's overall revenue...These estimates don't even take into account the back-breaking tax implications that could be triggered in the third year of the deal if the Knicks were to go over the salary cap. Two of MSG's

---

[23] Matthew Gee, my nephew, is now a point guard for his varsity basketball team.

[24] Debord, Guy. Section 16.

with a surprising first step, elevate and twist around the team's starting forward, and drop the ball in for a score. The UNH players look at each other with shocked expressions; their faces ask, *How did that just happen*? For the next two defensive plays, the starting guard retaliates by driving on me, but I steal the ball so he only grows angrier, embarrassed in front of his teammates, needing to salvage his pride and restore the norm of his athlete's unrelenting rugged individualism. We play each other with fierce moves, and because of the advantage he has from his blue chip players, my team loses. Still I end up outscoring him, and then a man wearing a sweat suit who has been standing on the edge of the court beckons to me. "You're really fast," he says. "Do you want to practice with the team?" I'm excited that the coach has noticed me, but I'm also busy adjusting to college life. As my mind leaps forward as it has before to basketball possibilities, I know that I don't want to warm the bench or be a practice player. Why give every regular hour to a sport and have to study during my spare

main revenue streams—ticket sales and deals with cable companies—are completely unaffected by Jeremy Lin, says Laura Martin, an analyst at Needham & Co. Cable...deals are locked in five years at a time, and season ticket sales are sold well in advance, regardless of the team's roster, she says.[25]

At 11 p.m. EST on Tuesday night, one hour before the New York Knicks needed to decide...the point guard's cell phone rang at his parents' home in Palo Alto, Calif. The call was from New York general manager Glen Grunwald and the conversation lasted no more than 30 seconds. Grunwald's message, Lin told SI.com, was simple and direct: "We wanted to keep you, but it couldn't work out. Tell your family I say hello, and good luck the rest of the way.[26]

One year sponsorships with Taiwan-based Maxxis International, a tire manufacturer, and Acer, Inc., the fourth largest computer maker, ended...Coca-cola Co. had placed large advertisements in Chinese at courtside of Madison Square Garden last season once Lin grabbed international attention.[27]

---

[25] Steven Russolillo and Johnathan Chang. "Analysts to Knicks: Dump Jeremy Lin." *Wall Street Journal*. July 17, 2012.

[26] Pablo S. Torre. "Lin Opens up about leaving Knicks; Honestly, I preferred New York." *Sportsillustrated.cnn.com*.

[27] Curis Eichelberger and Scott Soshnick. "Jeremy Lin's Departure to Houston Already Costing Knicks Money." *Bloomberg.com*. July 18, 2012.

time? My life needs to be the other way around. Since I aspire to be a professor, a veterinarian or a surgeon, I'm already aware that a lower grade point average will keep me out of contention for graduate schools. So I smile, hesitating, and as the coach pitches how he could use someone with my speed and leaping ability, the long shot possibility of beating out the starting guard and playing every game buzzes through me for a moment. The fantasy doesn't last, though, because where will it take me? I don't believe I can ever play in the NBA. I know how to win; I know the game, but without the advantage of height one has to be extraordinary like Nate "Tiny" Archibald who is the only man my height playing in the NBA. *Thanks, but I can't,* I say, and then I tell the coach, at least determining my own fate instead of having someone else tell me what I should do: "I played a lot in high school, so I know how much time it takes. It's not my game anymore. I'll watch from the stands. Good luck with your season."

Therefore as others act stunned by the emergence, the China likely played a role in his contract with the Houston Rockets, according to many observers. Many question whether the Knicks hadn't considered Lin as a major marketing connection to China, where the NBA has a hefty following...The point guard is launching a non-profit sports camp for children later this month (in China)... in the hopes that a few Chinese children will follow in Lin's footsteps.[28]

Interior Meta-Monologue #7:

Debord observes, The oldest social specialization, the specialization of power, is at the root of the spectacle."[29] So Houston's management was more global in its estimation and decision-making, no doubt due to their experience working with Yao Ming, and there are China's 300 million and more television viewers to consider. Lin's red Rockets 'jersey, emblazoned with his new No. 7 is already for sale. I'll be in Houston in 2013; tickets are expensive but one never knows. Lin's success reveals for me how little America has evolved as far as perception is concerned, and only fate can determine his Rocket future. But I suppose due to the power of the spectacle, that if one dresses up as Jeremy Lin for Hal-

---

28 Laurie Burkitt and Sandra Hu. "Jeremy Lin Pushes Fun Amid Gold Rush." *Wall Street Journal.Chinarealtimereport.* Aug. 9, 2012.

29 Debord, Guy. Section 23.

winning-streak and the talent of Jeremy Lin, I have been expectant all along, knowing it was simply a foregone conclusion and a matter of time until an Asian-American player would materialize and be talented enough to play in the NBA. I hold no deep regrets when it comes to basketball that have in any way ruined my outlook on life, but I admit to possessing a small amount of envy, wishing but not dreaming that I could have been the one who was tall and gifted enough, wondering what it would be like if it had been me.

loween, one will certainly, at least, be "recognized."

2012–2013 Update:

While some reporters labeled Lin as a "phenomenon," because of his slow start with the Houston Rockets, in his first game not playing alongside guard James Harden on Dec. 10th, Lin dropped in 38 points against the San Antonio Spurs.[30] It's clear that he can score wherever he plays; his Knicks' run wasn't a fluke. And now the Rockets are 20–14, and Lin's scoring average has risen to 14.2 ppg. Lin's fans await the playoffs, and at the very least, in front of the television, I'll be watching.

30 Franki Garcia. "Jeremy Lin News: Struggles Prove Houston Rockets Overpaid for Player who is No Superstar, Just All Hype" (Commentary). *Sportsworldreport.com*. Nov. 14, 2012.

Asians In The Library

n March of 2011, I watched what has now become the infamous video by Alexandra Wallace, a third-year political science major who, during finals week, shamelessly posted a Youtube rant about Asians in the library at UCLA. Her video instantly went viral on the Internet. Millions logged on and reacted with tolerance-based horror to her bashing monologue. Responses proliferated by the thousands, some dissenters distinguishing themselves by being more eloquent than others, and the most noteworthy voice—I think because of its artfulness—was the satiric *Ching Chong Asians in the Library Song* by Jimmy Wong, which has drawn, as of today, 4,094,967 viewers. Wallace's rant left me angry, so as I listened to Wong's song, I was hoping that my emotions would be soothed, and that I would, at some point, move on to other significant matters.

But for a year my mind continued to circle back and dwell on the dialogue between Wallace and Wong. Why did Wallace's words and her complaints create such a long-running backlash of online activity? Why did Jimmy Wong's sensitive yet humorous crooning receive so much attention? And why did I feel almost personally invested in what had been happening?

Alexandra Wallace's rant lasts a brief two minutes and fifty-two seconds, about the time it takes me to run a brisk half mile. She speaks from a dorm room, wearing a scanty, taut pink-trimmed top, inciting objection within moments by saying: "The problem is these hordes of Asian people that UCLA accepts into our school every single year, which is fine, but if you're going to come to UCLA then use American manners." Any listener instantly knows that Wallace is out of step, not part of the tolerant, more-enlightened generation she's supposed to belong to, while for a middle-aged Chinese-American like me, the word "hordes" and then the words "our school" bring to mind the anti-Chinese immigration laws and the exclusion mentality of California's racial politics during the 1860s. Wallace also made me think of the evolving history of enrollment policies at UCLA. Since Proposition 209 in California in 1996 banned state entities from using affirmative action, or since the admissions playing field was "leveled" by becoming determined by standardized test scores alone, Asian-Americans have emerged as frontrunners in West coast academia. UC Berkley's Asian population jumped from 37.3% in 1995 to 48.6% today, and at UCLA, Asians are now a majority at 37.12%. Wallace's old-school centrist view assumes that UCLA should be white. This was the reason why Caucasians protested affirmative action to begin with, but they had no idea that the policy's removal would lead to Asians being admitted in vast numbers.

Wallace's litany of complaints moves on like a filibuster:

> ...all the Asian people that live in all the apartments around me, their moms and their brothers and their sisters and their grandmas and their grandpas and their cousins and everybody that they know that they've brought from Asia with them, come here on the weekends to do their laundry, buy their groceries and cook their food for the week. It's, seriously, without fail. You will always see old Asian people running around this apartment complex every weekend. That's what they do.

> They don't teach their kids to fend for themselves.

I felt astonished that Wallace was striking down a core value of Asian-America by critiquing family togetherness. She was also inverting a major Asian route to gain independence by criticizing high scholastic achievement with the support of one's family, completely misunderstanding the reason for close-knit, multi-generational behavior.

What follows is the emotional center of Wallace's rant, for she remarks with an annoying whine that has the impact of trauma, commenting snidely about Asians talking on their cell phones in the library:

I'll be, like, deep into my studying, into my political science theories and arguments and all that stuff, getting it all down, like typing away furiously—blah blah blah—and then all of a sudden when I'm about to, like, reach an epiphany, over here from somewhere, 'Ooohh, ching chong ling long ting tong, ooohh.'

The underlying comic irony that Wallace will never be able to escape is the doubt that she is even capable of having a real epiphany, because she's ignorant enough to be so openly racist—and then there's her rendition of Chinese speech, which otherizes an entire race, casting it aside, for all purposes dismissing it, and in so doing she attains the level of Roland Barthes' definition in *Mythologies* of what otherizing is, which is to ultimately conquer or destroy. At the same time, Wallace is simplifying what is actually a complex tonal language by trying to parody it with an old singsong rhyme, and this type of broad stroke harkens back to stereotypical portrayals of Asians that used to dominate racist Hollywood movies. A viewer of Wallace's rant likely wonders, when was she born? What planet has she been living on? Was she raised in the 1950s?

Wallace presses the issue further, exclaiming about one Asian talking on a cell phone:

Are you freaking kidding me? In the middle of finals week? So being the polite, nice American girl that my momma raised me to be, I kinda just give him what anybody else would do, that kinda, like, (she puts her index finger up to her lips in a 'ssshh' motion) you know, it's a library, like, we're trying to study. Thanks!

And then it's the same thing five minutes later. But it's somebody else, you know. I swear they're going through their whole families, just checking on everybody from the tsunami thing.

At this point I could only wonder, how can this woman possibly be speaking openly like this? Not only was she assuming some farfetched superiority because she'd been raised by a white mother, but the idea of her being an exclusively American girl, or that her type of behavior must remain as the standard for everyone to uphold, struck me not only as outlandish but as disturbing. Could anyone really be so self-involved and insensitive toward the plight of families of tsunami victims, not to mention confusing what had occurred in Japan with the predominantly Chinese student body at UCLA? But this is life according to Alexandra Wallace, a former wannabe swimsuit model, lacking any civilized awareness, without any greater concern for the shrinking "postmodern" planet that we're all supposedly citizens of; she can't refrain from targeting, with her sense of entitlement, Asians in the library. And what other building or space on a college campus is more vital to scholarly upward mobility, to achieving the American dream? Yet without a moment of regret or reservation, she goes on to thank everyone for listening, and closes with a smug "and have a nice day."

Although loathing Alexandra Wallace's sense of privilege and her assumption of ownership of the library, I still think that she wasn't capable of anticipating the furor that she would cause. She can certainly be viewed as one of Asian America's strongest indications that having the first African-American President, Barrack Obama, fails—on so many levels—to signify that we are now part of an entirely enlightened post-racial nation. African-Americans have already been quite aware that deep fissures remain throughout the nation, and that for many, Martin Luther King, Jr.'s dream of racial equality is still nowhere near to being a reality. This was confirmed by the July 16, 2009 arrest of the nation's preeminent African-American scholar, Henry Louis Gates, who teaches at Harvard but was detained by police under suspicion of burglary while trying to enter his own Cambridge home. For me, Wallace's rant parallels the treatment Gates was subjected to; she reminds us that no matter how much another race believes it has attained, or no matter much how it believes it has progressed, there is still always the dominant status quo that will question one's right to belong.

What Wallace also proved, unfortunately, is that not only is racism still to be feared from law enforcement officers who profile, or Klu Klux Klansmen, or skinheads, but now racism can blatantly arise from what has been traditionally perceived as the innocuous "good girl", in this case, one who invokes how she was raised by her mother. Isn't this the kind of girl whom far too many in America have been conditioned by the media to desire or want to marry? Think Marilyn Monroe in her billowing white dress, posed indelibly above a steam grate, or picture Farrah Fawcett with her dazzling white smile and red swimsuit, permanently poster-emblazoned in the American male consciousness. Remember the bombshells Jayne Mansfield or Kim Novak? More recently, blondeness is exalted via Heidi Klum, Jessica Simpson, Jessica Alba, Britney Spears, and Kate Upton. Alexandra Wallace, of all things, raises the question: isn't blondness supposed to represent the locus of desire associated with wholesome youth, vitality, and sexuality? Isn't it an American truism that to be with a blonde is like a prize or a reward, something only those more masculine or wealthy or fortunate than others can attain?

I have thought back, and what I have remembered is that from 1982 to 1983, during my sophomore and junior years at the University of New Hampshire, I ensconced myself every night until closing time on the uppermost floor of the Diamond Library, reading English Literature—

the Bronte sisters for one course—as well as classic American novels for another: *As I Lay Dying, The Country of the Pointed Firs, The Great Gatsby, My Antonia,* and *A Farewell to Arms.* The library became a refuge, a sanctum from roommates and parties, and since I had been an athlete in high school (running cross-country, playing basketball, and running track) which demanded every extra hour, now my mind was compensating, catching up for what I imagined were mental deficiencies. And I have remembered that since my older brother was a child prodigy, a classical pianist, there was always music resounding throughout the house, the volume at times deafening, never conducive to reading; in the library I was also learning about quiet and where silence can lead one's mind and thoughts. I discovered the far-reaching realms of literature in the library, contemplating who I was by comparing myself to the characters in the worlds created by each novel's author. I would have happily stayed long past closing time, so I can imagine how I would have felt if someone like Alexandra Wallace had told me I shouldn't be there or had to leave.

Jimmy Wong's video response to Alexandra Wallace features him singing solo with an acoustic guitar, sometimes utilizing four concurrent screens to show images of him singing lead, singing his own backup chorus, hand clapping, or rhythm shaking. When interviewed by Melissa Block on NPR's *All Things Considered,* Wong speaks of needing a couple of days to write the *Ching Chong Asians in the Library Song,* which is a mock seduction from the start.

Wong's song opens with nerdy self-deprecation; he pretends not to speak English well, laying on a thick accent, satirizing Wallace's characterization of Asians. He becomes, to a heightened degree, the Asian "other" she makes the Asians in the library out to be. His eyes appear serious and he bows his head, but the real humor commences when he starts to speak enticingly:

Oh, Alexandra Wallace. Damn, girl. You so feisty. You
so feisty they should call you Alexandra Great Wall
Ace. And don't pretend I didn't see you watching me
talking on my phone yesterday all sexy—ching chong
wing wong. Baby, it's all just code. It's the way I tell the
ladies it's time to get funky.

Underlying all of this is the ingenious subtext of hearing an Asian
man speak provocatively to a blonde white woman, which I cannot recall hearing or seeing as of late with any regularity on television or at
the movies. Here Wong is not the typically emasculated Asian male, but
a young man restructuring any perceived hierarchy of gender or racial
desire; his speaking out, satire or not, is a form of rebellion. What ap-
peals most to me is how he mocks how he's supposed to desire Wallace,
while it's blatantly obvious that he doesn't really want her. He rejects
America's elevation of blonde beauty. Wong launches into singing the
first verse without an accent, sometimes lifting his eyebrows dramati-
cally, and Wallace remains the object of seduction:

I hope one day you can meet my mother, brothers,
sisters, grandmothers, grandpas, and cousins, oh, cuz
what they're really doing on those Friday nights is
showing me how to cook and dress, cuz baby I want to
take you out and blow your freaking mind.

The chorus follows, laced with its own insults to contradict Wallace's rant: "And underneath the pounds of makeup and your baby blue
eyes/I know there's a lot of pain and hurt/for such a big brain to spend
all night studying poly sci."

The rest of the chorus is Wong's revisionist interpretation of what
her racist portrayal of Chinese speech means to him; he takes the standard of racial debasement that she derives from Chinese language, and
appropriates it for his own riff of mocking humor:

I pick up my phone and sing: Ching chong, it means I
love you Ling long, I really want you Ting tong, I don't

actually know what that means. Ching chong, it's never ending Ling long, my head is spinning Ting tong,
still don't know what that means.

Wong's accentuating of Wallace's crude imitation of Asian speech in
the chorus— her "ching chong ling long ting tong"—also prompts Melissa Block in her NPR interview to speculate whether "ching chong ling
long ting tong" might "become part of our cultural lexicon" or like "a
shorthand" for something. As Block suggested, the words have indeed
become part of our language; you can now find *ching chong ling long*
being used in a myriad of online postings and even printed on T-shirts
being sold for tsunami relief.

Wong maintains the high level of inverse satire, for his song returns
to spoken word verse and becomes humorously seductive again: "Oohh,
Alex. I just want to take my phone out and talk dirty to you all day long. But
I know you're busy cramming all those big hard theories and arguments."
He gives the camera a sly wink, and then the second verse commences:

You ain't that polite, nice American girl that your
momma raised you to be so when you reach that
epiphany—wait, are you freaking kidding me?—if
you have an epiphany every single time you study that
probably means you're doing something wrong but I
like it when you're wrong.

The song unleashes racial protest here, as well as irritation directed
at Wallace's assumed authority and intelligence, and then the chorus is
repeated before Wong speaks enticingly one last time, amplifying the
seduction with phallic sexual humor:

It's alright, Alexandra, I know you know nothing about
tsunamis I just want to make sure you know that it's
not a type of sushi but I came here to say that I'm actually Chinese and that's a whole 'nother country, and
it's bigger yeah, way bigger, but when it comes to love,
Alexandra there are no boundaries.

Wong closes with a "Thank you" in the formal Chinglish voice of the opening, faintly echoing Wallace's "and have a nice day." During his NPR interview, he describes his song as containing "sharp wit" but downplays his reaction to Wallace by remarking, "I was pretty offended at first, but then I realized this is just someone going on a rant, and we've all done that before." He adds that his song, like Wallace's rant, is never really hostile, and claims that he would "love to meet her for coffee and give her a big hug."

While praising Wong's non-violent creative response, however, reporter Dave Pell on NPR's *Technology Blog* links Wallace to cyber bullies, reminding us "just how easy it is to spread hate in the Internet age."

Overall, a discernible element of tragedy lurks beneath Wong's use of satire to respond to Wallace, the feeling of laughing and crying at the same time, which I think is the most significant factor contributing to why the song has drawn and captivated so many listeners. Wallace's rant does sadden our emotional human landscape. And while the insulting lyrics in Wong's song are payback or barbs for Wong's being part of the intended target of Wallace's derogatory generalizations, why couldn't he just admit his irritation and feel justified?

In the aftermath of Alexandra Wallace's online rant, in her real day-to-day life, she and her family received death threats. So she soon issued an apology, stating: "I cannot explain what possessed me to approach the subject as I did, and if I could undo it, I would... For those who cannot find it within them to accept my apology, I understand." She simultaneously announced her withdrawal from UCLA. One recent article suggests her video was a publicity stunt because her career as a political science major apparently held no more promise than Sarah Palin's infamous bridge to nowhere. A glimpse at Wallace's bathing suit modeling photos, which are posted prominently online, shows what appears to be fearless self-promotion; Wallace stares down the camera like she knows what she's doing and thrives upon it, like she possesses great self awareness. If her rant was for publicity, however, it certainly backfired, because she branded herself with a "racist" label, and what racists do we know of who have managed successful career comebacks?

Examining Greek history, we can find that Wallace is akin to Julian the Apostate, who, after the reign of Constantine, reinstated the pagan religion of Rome as the state religion, and so the protection of minority Christians—like any security Asian-Americans might have felt at UCLA—was nullified. We could view her symbolically, then, as a sign of one historical tradition stubbornly refusing to give way to another. If I apply a more contemporary lens, she reminds me of the late Governor George Wallace of Alabama, who was the face of modern Southern segregation. One of the more horrific quotes attached to him is: "Segregation now, segregation tomorrow, segregation forever." When he recanted later in life, history certainly didn't lessen its judgment of how awful he was.

While we can easily recognize that Alexandra Wallace's rant was a clear overestimation of her own power, what her actions ultimately indicate is that not only can racism spring from what American popular culture has repeatedly tried to tell us is the simplest, most desirable iconic identity—the attractive blonde female—but also that the assumed privilege of white America, its once clearly dominant unjust advantage, is becoming diluted, fractured, and strained, possibly nearing a breaking point.

Thanks to Alexandra Wallace, America must acknowledge that the wholesome blonde California girl in the white swimsuit may no longer represent good vibrations. Asian America's empowered voice is found in the thousands of responses and millions of hits for the clever croon-er, Jimmy Wong, the face of a race in retaliation, one that is no longer the silent minority that many of the status quo would like it to remain. Wallace probably wasn't the last vacuous blonde to protest Asian suc-cess by trying to subvert an entire ethnic group's version of the Ameri-can dream. So we should caution our mothers, brothers, sisters, grand-mothers, grandpas, and cousins, because Wallace's rant is the portent of more Asian-vilifying times ahead. As for me, I'll be doing my part by reading in coffee shops, parks, museums, airports, on trains, and in libraries, forever staying visible.

The Real New South

Two hours southeast of Atlanta lies Milledgeville. The town sits right in the center of Georgia and is part of rural Baldwin County, the soil red clay, the streets once walked by Klansmen, and what was once the world's largest psychiatric institution—Central State Hospital—hovers on the town's outskirts. If any true consideration can be given toward reimagining the South as the "New South", I suggest one starting place is whether an Asian-American, someone not already part of the predominant African-American and white binary, can permanently reside here.

Seven years ago, I walked to the main intersection at Hancock and Wayne Streets, looked both ways, and observed that the primary businesses extended only a block in all four directions of the compass. Could such a small town (officially designated as a city) become my home? Earlier that day I had gazed almost reverentially, like a tourist in awe, at grand historic homes with broad white columns; black iron plaques in front of each address displayed the dates of construction and what venerable families had lived in each house and for how long, most of the initial years being from c. 1800 to 1830. The enduring acknowledgements prompted the thought that the myth of the Old South was still very powerful, and that such a myth would not give way easily to attempts at being rewritten and recast as a part of the "New South", which would include the likes of me.

Since her family lived in Atlanta, my wife and I eventually chose to put aside our fears and move from our home in Houston, Texas to Milledgeville, the antebellum capital of Georgia. I told myself that my presence as part of the 1.5% Asian population of 18,000 Milledgeville residents would matter and be significant. I hoped to become a racial pioneer.

To learn the town required knowing the streets better. What I discovered, like a diligent surveyor, is that heading southbound and proceeding on Highway 441 (otherwise known as Columbia Street), national retail and restaurant chains abound. There's a glut comprised of Wal-Mart, Mc-Donald's, Arby's, Wendy's, Ruby Tuesdays, Starbucks, Walgreens, CVS, Ace Hardware, Lowes, Dollar General, Kroger, Blockbuster, Office Max, and K-Mart, along with Honda, Toyota, and Chevrolet dealerships. The large signage and sense of uniformity is ugly and somewhat numbing. You have to ignore the longest stretch of highway to keep from getting a headache, but to me this retail zoning is also a sign of the outside world being kept out, of the town controlling its identity.

But what is that identity? The subsequent stretch, closer to Milledgeville, is filled with hard-times financial profiteers. Crammed together, in the space of less than a mile, are: Speedee Cash, Pawn and Wholesale, Rent-A-Center ("No Credit Needed"), Titlebucks Title Pawn ("We Give More!"), Spires Auto Sales ("No Credit Check!"), Penny's Title & Pawn, Northside Loans, and finally the offices of Get Cash Fast ("Tax Refund Loan"). Two massive billboards along the road proclaim: "Titlebucks Title Pawn, We Give More! No Credit Check!" and "Wilksinson Title Pawn, No Credit Check! We Loan More For Less!" It is no coincidence that a sizable section of lower class African-American homes are adjacent to these high-interest predatory businesses, and the irony does not escape me that one of the cross streets is Martin Luther King, Jr. Drive. Right after this, railroad tracks cross the highway, which then thins into a single-lane road.

Soon some of the older historic homes begin to appear, and reaching the Georgia College campus, it's immediately apparent that the town proper does not allow any large-scale chains. This is quaint, idyllic small-town America with antique shops and restaurants called Buffington's, The Brick, Velvet Elvis, Aubri Lane's, Kuroshika, and Amici's. The independently owned Blackbird coffee shop, Antebellum Inn bed-and-breakfast, Bayne's Army Navy, and the Whipple Office Equipment Company also exemplify small private businesses. The Baldwin County Courthouse, Milledgeville City Hall, the U.S. Post Office, and a visitor's center are also located downtown, where the city slogan, "Capitals, Columns & Culture", appears proudly on signs and in storefront windows.

Heading south on Elbert Street, where Route 112 becomes Vinson Highway, the landscape alters rapidly and becomes much less prosperous, the houses situated close together, many with rusted tin roofs, some boarded up, with peeling paint and weedy yards and longstanding "For Sale" signs. Trash obscures some of the lawns, and a trailer park has been bestowed the ill-fitting name, Chateau Village. The road soon leads by Central State Hospital; almost all of the brick buildings are abandoned and decaying, the windows still barred, the mood haunting and eerie like the set of a horror film. Rivers State Prison follows—it is said to have served as the inspiration for Milledgeville native Flannery O'Connor's character, The Misfit, in her short story "A Good Man Is Hard to Find." On water towers, turkey vultures perch en masse, as unpleasing to the eye as gargoyles. Yet this part of town is where I ended up living for my first year in Georgia, in a small rented house off Route 112 on Perry Drive.

Real estate agents do not show perspective white buyers this neighborhood because most of the residents are from lower income brackets. Nevertheless, my wife and I lived there on a modest black and white street where I was the only Asian to be found for miles. The year of renting there and learning the geography of Milledgeville confirmed what I had believed while growing up in New York: Although one can discover many stories of pockets of other races residing in the South—

even of Asians living in Mississippi—the Old South was, by and large, black and white, segregated by law, and the legacies of this binary still abound, although politicians in the past, and as of late, would like to claim otherwise.

My readings tell me that the phrase "New South" was originally used directly after the Civil War to describe a South with an economy no longer tied to slavery, an economy that would rival that of the rest of the industrialized nation. In an 1889 edition of the *Atlanta Constitution*, Editor Henry Grady gives a defiant speech filled with excessive regional pride:

> "We have got the biggest marble-cutting establishment
> on earth…We have got a half-dozen woolen mills, and
> iron mines, and iron furnaces, and iron factories. We
> are coming to meet you. We are going to take a noble
> revenge, as my friend, Mr. Carnegie, said last night, by
> invading every inch of your territory with iron, as you
> invaded ours twenty-nine years ago."

During the Civil Rights Movement in the 1960s, racial conflict renewed the national view of the South's backward image because of the insistence by many for compulsory legal segregation; notwithstanding, in 1957, governors like LeRoy Collins of Florida, known as a spokesman for the "New South", were promoting an open-minded attitude towards integration. Others like Caroll Campbell Jr. of South Carolina and Lamar Alexander of Tennessee followed, embracing progressive ideas on education, supporting economic growth, and furthering integrationist goals.

More recently, the "New South" has been heralded as more global, more cosmopolitan, and ethnically diverse. Prior to the current economic recession, there was also a reported economic boom in the South, while the Midwest suffered tremendous job losses. As of 2014, Atlanta claims the third-most Fortune 500 companies in the nation, trailing only behind Houston and New York. In this "New South", banking and auto manufacturing are on the rise, and one of the more humorous expressions I have heard, inspired by the BMW plant now located near Greenville, South Carolina, is how BMW stands for *Bubba Makes Wheels*.

But on Vinson Highway in my real "New South" (some local residents say—with a particular gleam of pride in their eyes as if knowing a greater truth—that they're from "The Dirty South"), Milledgeville builds no new parks and fails to invest in the rejuvenation of large-scale public spaces. The development of new businesses is rarely encouraged, unlike downtown and due north of the city. Young African-American men often walk out into the road, brazenly straddling the solid white stripe of the breakdown lane, frequently causing drivers to swerve. This rebellious gesture is an expression of pride and ownership, of masculinity and control, and of frustration over institutionalized poverty. The low, one's street bravado, trumps the high of any vehicle of status, defies anyone regardless of income. Who owns the road? Only these young African-American men do. It is a constant declaration that all is not well. As saddened as I am by this sight on Vinson Highway, I have observed the same behavior while driving through the rest of rural Georgia, parts of Florida, Alabama, and South Carolina, where economic segregation—like an old sore—still exists.

Of course the same kind of division can be found in the North, but the North does not insist on renaming itself. And in terms of ethnic diversity, as far as our Asian population is concerned, whether on the downtown streets of Milledgeville or at Georgia College, where I'm an English professor, I often ponder how I see fewer Asians in a year than I glimpse in an afternoon at any urban airport. My first year here, I kept my own "Asian watch" throughout Milledgeville and on campus; the total number was thirty-six. This left me feeling isolated, like some kind of rare bird or endangered species. Georgia College, as well, is classified as a PWI, *Primarily White Institution*. Only 12% of the students are students of color. Minority recruitment, the administration says, must be a priority.

~

The predominant myth of the Old South, of course, is not of integration, but of the South's stately traditions that evoke connotations of grace and elegance and refinement, with specific behaviors like Southern charm and hospitality. Think mansions, porches, and being offered sweet tea or mint juleps. But too much of the old grandeur was interwoven with slave plantation economies and therefore doomed to failure. In terms of the greater consciousness now, or what lies within the minds of the "New South" citizenry, the Old South's unfavorable racial premises, practices, and principles are (except within the mindset of an ignorant, radical, out-of-step minority), fortunately, dead and gone, buried like a plantation patriarch. So we have the "New South" that I consider becoming a part of, which is clearly not a reality because of the lingering economic segregation, but more like an ideal or a guiding principle.

Southern hospitality endures, less associated now with the grandeur of the Old South but regularly promoted by individuals. Unparalleled graciousness still exists, apart from all the flawed premises of the Confederacy. My father-in-law, Bobby Dodd Jr., son of legendary Georgia Tech football coach, Bobby Dodd (who was actually Robert Lee Dodd, named for General Lee), could not have been more welcoming. That an Asian man married his white daughter has never mattered, my Chinese background never a topic early on for discussion. We like to watch football together and go fishing; six years ago after he happened to catch a nice speckled trout, I asked for his daughter's hand in marriage. He has continually offered to help decorate our houses with furniture from the Dodd family antique business. My mother-in-law, Margie Dodd, encouraged my wife and I to be married in her backyard garden in Decatur, and on the day of the wedding, she graciously welcomed my entire Asian-American family into her home.

Likewise, in Milledgeville, the people who work the counter at the Goodie Gallery, a local bakery, noticed my affinity for custard pie and told me that I need only call ahead in the morning, and they will bake a fresh pie and save it for me. A retired conservation officer, Marion Nelson, allows me to hunt undisturbed on a large parcel of his property; I go for the peace and quiet, watching wildlife, rarely taking a shot. Along the same vein, John Baum, a descendant of an old Milledgeville family, has taken me fishing on the local waters of Lake Sinclair for several seasons. A longtime friend, the African-American poet, Sean Hill—whom I met while studying at the University of Houston—grew up in Milledgeville. After he read here recently, his family invited me over for a steak and crab dinner.

In spite of all the good there is in the South, I am continually asked about how much racism I have experienced. On my first visit to a local bank, carrying my driver's license, Social Security card, passport, newly-signed lease, utility bill with my name on it, and a copy of my birth certificate, I asked to open a checking account. The woman at the customer service desk eyed the passport and proclaimed, "You can't open an account with that!"

She was rushing to judgment, assuming I was one of Georgia College's international students, newly-arrived from abroad. Forget that my grandfather came to the United States in 1908. Normally I am not quick to speak up in public, but that morning at the bank, defensive because I was uncertain about making my way in the Deep South (there is even a local realtor here called Deep South), I said in a loud and masculine harsh voice, "Why can't I open a checking account here? I was born in the United States, I have my birth certificate, my Georgia driver's license, and I was just hired at the local college as an English professor. What does it take?"

Silence fell upon the entire bank. The clerk proceeded to apologize. Her racism sprang from ignorance and presumption, a reminder that nothing can be taken for granted on a day-to-day basis for a person of color, not even in contemporary America. Likewise, each semester when I enter a classroom for the first time, especially if I'm teaching a core class like World Literature to non-English majors, I confront apprehension on students' faces, their nervousness almost palpable about whether or not I'll be capable of speaking clear English. A time or two I haven't said anything for a moment, smiling to myself, enjoying the students' discomfort, letting them dwell in the bias of their limited perspectives, until finally I'll say a few introductory words, and hearing their relief escape in long breaths, I'll shake my head and wonder—what if I assumed they were all as ignorant and racist as some of their fellow Southerners?

In April of 2007, after the tragic shooting spree at Virginia Tech in Blacksburg, VA, I received a telephone call from the Georgia College newspaper, *The Colonnade*, asking if I would make a comment about the shooting. I wondered what possible association or connection the student reporter could be making between me—a Chinese-American, hard-working, well-adjusted, 44-year-old creative writing professor— and Seung-Hui Cho—a Korean-American senior undergraduate creative writing major who had been declared mentally ill by a Virginia Special Justice and accused of stalking two female students—who had just shot and killed 32 people and wounded many others, committing the deadliest shooting rampage by a single gunman, on or off campus, in U.S. history? Why had the reporter contacted me, instead of another creative writing program faculty member? Was the reporter asking if I knew what it was like to go mad, to become murderous and crazy, in a small Southern town? I told the reporter that for an overarching statement he should speak to Martin Lammon, the director of our creative writing program, who is a white male from Ohio.

On another level, if I happen to be eating in a local Chinese restaurant like Lieu's Peking, or if I've ventured out for sushi at Little Tokyo, I'll glance up and notice white people staring, marveling at how deftly I use chopsticks. They can't help themselves; it's like a form of voyeurism, of unfettered curiosity about what seems foreign and exotic—right there in front of them. More often than not, I'm the only Asian person eating in an Asian restaurant here. My presence is likely a barometer of whether the food is good or not; I often joke with the restaurant owners that I should be charging them for my endorsement.

All of this is dwarfed, though, by what I heard downtown one morning. I asked an older, white barber about what he thought of Barack Obama's presidential candidacy. The man erupted, his voice spewing that he was glad as hell they'd gotten that bitch Hillary Clinton out of there, but that Obama was nothing but a slick-talkin' nigger who belonged to a heathen church. Here was the ugly Old South, still alive, like a boxer with a swollen eye, beaten and nearly down for the count, but still able to throw a vicious punch. Here was the underlying hate lurking beneath the "Bless your hearts" and the "Yes, sirs" and "No, sirs", simmering just below the surface of the unparalleled icon of the Southern Gentleman. Southern hospitality notwithstanding, I have not returned to the man for a haircut.

Racism, I am glad to say, will not determine whether I remain in Milledgeville. I believe my sense of cultural isolation will be the most crucial factor. Since we moved to Georgia to be closer to my wife's family, I was partly adhering to the Chinese tradition of living for one's family, rather than prioritizing one's individual needs. Another aspect of being Chinese-American for me is that I grew up in a Chinese restaurant family; my grandfather owned and ran a Chinese restaurant in the Bronx and held interests in others in Chinatown, New York, so food occupies an important part of my cultural memory.

My father grew up cooking in our family's restaurant, and each weekend during my youth he cooked traditional Cantonese meals. But here, the restaurant voted Best Chinese by Milledgeville residents is Lieu's Peking, which is located in a shopping mall. The first time I met the young Asian man, Bob, who runs the front counter, I knew he wasn't Chinese. He told me that no one had ever questioned his ethnicity before and admitted, with a downward look of embarrassment, that he is Korean and grew up in Des Moines, Iowa. The menu at Lieu's quickly reveals to the knowing eye that they don't serve "authentic" Chinese cuisine, but what I call Chinese junk food or palatable cuisine for less adventurous white people. There are the predictable sweet and sour dishes, chow meins, lo meins, egg rolls, won ton soups, and varieties of fried rice. When I long for the food of my childhood, I ask Bob, "Do you have any *juk* or *chow fun* today?" He tells me that they don't serve that, meaning they don't cook rice porridge or flat rice noodles. Once in a sarcastic mood, I asked, "How about some steamed sea bass with ginger?" Bob replied that he couldn't make that here, and then he looked at me as if I was being far too unreasonable. I suppose, to him, that I was, but I have returned time and again to his restaurant, because I know that, like most of us, he is just trying to make a living, offering the familiar dishes most of his customers will eat.

Still, Lieu's Peking is indicative of the potential difficulty of my staying in the "New South". In the same way that the menu is watered down and authenticity is not a priority, if I remain here, I, too, will be expected to keep subtracting more and more of my true self.

To find authentic Chinese food these days, I must travel two and half hours to the north side of Atlanta, to a restaurant called Canton Cooks; this is where I have to drive for Chinese New Year, or even just to eat *dim sum* (little steamed dumplings) during the weekend. While living in Houston, I frequented a restaurant in one of the two Chinatowns there, Ocean Palace, for *dim sum* with Asian friends up to three times a month. I ate weekly at a place called Canton Seafood five minutes from my home. Once after catching a limit of flounder in the Texas Gulf, I brought two five-pound flounders on ice to Canton Seafood, and the owner, Sam Siew, in the spirit of celebrating fresh food, had his chef prepare both fish in the restaurant's large steamer. When the fish were brought out, infused with slices of ginger and scallions and served Chinese style, head and all, upon decorative silver platters, I beamed, sated with joy.

When I tell someone in Georgia that I grew up in New York, they remark, harking back to the old divide between North and South, either in a casual or more serious tone, "Oh, you're a Yankee." What intrigues me about this is that I have never felt responsible or to blame for any of the longstanding geographic confrontation, or for any of the racism and mistreatment between blacks and whites. My immigrant roots separate me from this tragic history; Chinese-Americans didn't contribute to slavery. In fact, while Africans were forcefully being brought here, Chinese who wanted to emigrate became the object of anti-interracial marriage laws and deportation campaigns, particularly in the 1800s in California, where slogans arose like "The Chinese Must Go!"

While I've already recounted some of the racism I experience from whites, at the same time I'm constantly surprised by African-Americans, who, upon hearing that I was born and raised in America, make offhand remarks like, "Oh, so you're basically white." Their inherent assumption that I would want to think of myself as "white" strikes me as silly. Why would I want to be white, especially in the South, when that association here includes intense racism and the history of slavery and lynching? More importantly, why would I want to deny my own Chinese history and culture?

I think that those African-Americans who like to assume that I have white privileges, or the upper hand of lighter skin pigmentation, aren't aware that some whites, especially in the academic arena I work in, view me as a fierce source of competition, fearing I'll match the stereotypical Asian prodigy, or be the diligent hard-working immigrant.

One white male writer once complained to me in a jealous tone, "I wish I had a cultural background like yours to draw upon!"

I replied, "I think you have plenty of models for white success, like Hemingway, Faulkner, and Fitzgerald, and later on, well, how about Raymond Carver, Richard Ford, and Tobias Wolff? And now there's Jonathan Franzen. I think white men can still do just fine."

While I do consider myself hard-working, which stems from my family's original blue collar Toisanese farming roots in China, my determination stems more from a desire to live the most involved writing and teaching life possible, for the sake of wanting to fully explore the life of the mind. So for me, being Asian in the "New South" means occupying a unique space, a territory of my own, neither black nor white. While my features often serve as ethnic camouflage because whites will often unknowingly make severe racist comments about African-Americans in my presence, believing I'll remain complicit, or that I might hold the same beliefs, when I hear prejudice, I abruptly cut ties. And although some African-Americans believe I have advantages because my complexion is lighter, or supposedly more acceptable, and might also view me as a competitor vying for limited claims to minority status, they have not walked far enough in my shoes, and would certainly be surprised to know how much we have in common, as different as we are.

Time, I have learned, seems to pass more slowly in central Georgia; in fact there is almost a sense of timelessness. The seasons in other parts of the country are far more defined and distinct; here I endure the cold bleak grayness of winter from January to March—without any adhering snow—followed by the warmer weather of April and May, and then there is the blazing, stifling heat of summer from June to September. From October to December the leaves barely change, so spectacular foliage and below freezing nights are only a memory. One consequence of this lack of strong seasonal distinction is that there isn't always a feeling of urgency; I've become disconnected from all of the feelings and associations that used to warn or signal me that a year was passing. Sometimes I've felt suspended in time, since my mind and body used to be set according to repeated rituals, like the first day of trout season in upstate New York. As a younger man, on the first day of April I would drive to a stream or river and fish, bundled up in the thickest jacket and hat and gloves, even if the banks were blanketed with the thickest snow and the pools were edged with ice.

After our first year of house renting on the south side of Milledgeville, we moved and bought a house in Carrington Woods on Oliver Hardy Lake, just off Highway 441, on the way into town. The house had been owned by only one family and had not been renovated since being built in the 1960s. Some of Milledgeville's more well-to-do citizens had lived on Pine Valley Road, but over time most of the upper class had passed away or moved further north, so now Carrington Woods was more lower and middle class. To my surprise, on our street I discovered African-American families, an Indian family, a Mexican family, and many white families. There were older neighbors, too: a retired white couple to our left, and a ninety-four-year-old retired woman to our right. For me, the diversity of the street embodied what the "New South" might become. So while Milledgeville is arranged in a way that seems to assign poverty to the south, our new and diverse street was, for a time, a precedent, or a peaceful futuristic symbol of potential.

We lived on Pine Valley Road for four years, but when the recession hit, crime escalated. An organizational meeting was held at City Hall to form Neighborhood Watch committees. My ninety-four-year-old neighbor, who was deaf without her hearing aid, as well as succumbing to Alzheimer's disease, fell victim to two burglaries within a year. The first thief simply kicked down a door while she was still in her house. Men who were supposedly fishing on a small nearby piece of city property, a highway drainage creek, were using the spot as an access point to trespass and break into as many vulnerable homes as possible. Out of concern for the elderly retirees on both sides of me, I attended the city hall meeting and spoke, requesting "No Fishing" signs, citing prevention as more important than taking action after more crime occurred. I did not call for a ban on all public fishing on Oliver Hardy Lake, but only for signs at two locations. Over two hundred neighborhood residents were in attendance, and when my request received the largest round of applause, city council members assured me they would contact the city lawyer. Signs would then be posted. Up until that point, I had never participated in a democratic process to such a public extent, or felt as much a part of the Milledgeville community.

In my search for metaphors to describe what being part of the "New South" means, I have considered the mother in Jumpa Lahiri's novel, *The Namesake*, who dreams and sees her being an immigrant as akin to being pregnant, always being expectant and noticed. There is Flannery O'Connor's story "The Displaced Person," in which a Polish immigrant, Guzac, has been working on a farm and is run over and crushed by a tractor, because the farm's owner would rather that he feel beholden to her than ever leave. Guzac—if we apply O'Connor's sense of Orthodox Catholicism to the story—is Christ-like, an ultimate martyr figure, suffering for us all. I'm not inclined to compare my relocating to the South to pregnancy or religious ascension, but I would like to draw some parallels from what my mentor, James McPherson, has written about Ralph Ellison.

McPherson discusses in his essay, "Gravitas," about seeking to define Ellison's sense of being an American by how Aenas, in Virgil's *The Aeneid*, leaves Troy bearing his father, Ancheses, on his back. At the same time, Aeneas holds his son, Ascanius, by the hand and leads a small community of people who will centuries later lay the foundation for the *communitas* of Rome. Virgil, in writing the *Aeneid* to Augustus, teaches that it is piety toward the ancestors, towards the gods, and toward the family and community that has in the past, and will in the future, keep Rome vital. When man is in harmony with all these forces, McPherson writes, he may have "weight" and "consequence"—the intrinsic quality called "gravitas".

By comparing Ellison to Aneas, McPherson points out that Ellison was by no means a Tom, nor a mythologized literary wanderer and icon, nor a fatted calf, but a human being, someone who lived his life with an unwavering style and a recognizable commitment to the experiment and ideals of American democracy.

Though I will never possess the *gravitas* of Ellison, I aspire to have piety toward my ancestors, my family, and my community. My move to the South, if successful, might also be viewed as a sign of what is possible for the *communitas* of America. Can the "New South" eventually lay claim to white, black, and yellow (as well as red and brown)?

Much has also been written about Ellison going to the territory, about his being the only African-American member of the Century Club in New York and being rebuked by his own people for it. This shows the risks of being a man who aspired to journey from his Oklahoma lower class roots to the highbrow status of a member of a New York institution. My move to the South, by contrast, has required relinquishing a vibrant Houston literary, visual arts, and music scene, which has been replaced by the more blue collar pleasures of not only hunting and fishing, but also eating fried catfish lunches for $6.75 at Polly's Café in nearby Macon, or going hiking upon national forest land in nearby Bartram Forest. And if I am repeatedly contemplating a belief in American democracy, staying in the "New South" for me involves, I suppose, constantly asking the question of whether to endure cultural isolation for the sake of being a part of an evolving American idealism, rather than living where that democracy already feels more fully realized. To stay requires my having to want to say, "I was one of the first longtime Asians in Milledgeville," long before being able to say, "I was one of many."

Last April in 2010, we moved for a third time, but to the far north side of Baldwin County because of the increase in crime and because of how the recession had caused many more houses to become affordable on Lake Sinclair. My wife and I wanted to raise our newborn daughter on the water. I looked forward to taking her fishing, swimming, boating, and to feeling steadier breezes, welcoming any relief from the perilous Southern summer heat. The north side of the county was where robust development and fancier construction had been occurring for the past decade because of all the lakefront lots and undivided property. I had not, however, fully considered the implications of race when we purchased our new home.

I learned, to my displeasure, that almost all of the houses on the water were owned by whites. Integration seemed nonexistent. Entirely absent. One could almost believe that race was not something on peoples' minds at all. But when I took my boat, a Carolina Skiff, out to explore the shorelines, I noticed statues of African-American fishing boys on one dock after another. These statues, while "cute" or merely decorative to some, can be thought of as being as derogatory as lawn jockeys. They also perpetuate the stereotype of African-American laziness, the phrase and slur combined in "nigger fishing", of being a black boy and sitting and wanting to do nothing rather than being able to do something. I have wanted, since I first noticed these statues, to steal them all some night and sink them to the lake bottom, to have the pleasure of causing every ignorant or racist owner dismay. And these statues almost make me want to move back closer to town, back to Pine Valley Road. Living further out also means I don't frequent in-town restaurants as often, so I'm no longer an Asian man mixing as frequently as before with African-Americans and whites.

~

Why stay in the predominantly white area in the "New South?" I think, once again, that I'm being a racial pioneer, and I would like to suppose that, in some small way, like Ralph Ellison, I am defying expectations and have now gone to my own Century Club.

And if I stay in Milledgeville for good, this also requires that I face the ultimate question: Would I want to die here? What would that entail? In Chinese tradition, one's death should be preceded by having children, by living for family, and by making sure one's name continues. While I have two daughters, my youngest brother has two sons, so the Gee family name has never been a concern. Yet my memory of Chinatown funeral parlors is that they are steeped in tradition, preserving the practice of very distinct rituals. At a Chinese wake, pungent incense is burned to reinforce the sadness of the occasion, and coins are given in little packets of white paper so that a mourner can buy something sweet later to be sure to recall a happier time or a more pleasant memory of the deceased. We also regularly leave items like cigarettes or bottles of rice wine on burial plots, or we burn paper money there so the deceased will have plenty to spend in the afterlife. We might even place a whole simmered chicken by the gravestone so that the departed will have something delicious and more substantial to eat, as if to signify that there is never a last meal.

In Milledgeville, there are white and African-American funeral homes, one aptly named White Columns—you can guess who's buried there—and another is the People's Funeral Home, which sounds more down home and inviting, certainly more civil. But being neither black nor white, I remain unsure. If I stay in the "New South" until the end, and don't follow traditional Chinese burial customs, won't my spirit become lost? My cultural sense of being further diluted? I think that I'd prefer to trust the Wah Wing Sang Funeral Parlor on Mulberry Street in Chinatown, New York that buried my grandfather; they should take care of my remains. My body would have to be shipped north. So can I ever truly call the "New South" home?

Nevertheless, I stay on, like a guest at a decent hotel. Time passes slowly. I try not to think of the morning at Hartsfield Airport in Atlanta when a license and boarding pass inspector, upon seeing that I was from Milledgeville, asked me, referring to Central State Hospital's heyday, "Isn't that where all the crazy people are?"

Hoping that I wasn't one of the deranged, trying to stay upbeat, wanting to continue avoiding any association with shooting sprees, and considering myself as part of the grand experiment of democracy from now until I die, I told him, "Oh yes, you're right."

Echocardiography

I lifted my three-year-old daughter, Willa, onto my shoulders, and then we continued up the hill to take in the view of the Georgia pines and perhaps spot a deer or the great-horned owl that had swooped and soared skyward there a few days before. I was enthused by the leisurely morning, but soon my chest tightened, my heart beating far too fast. *Something's wrong*, I said to my friend, Sean Hill, who was hiking with us. I described the quickening of my heart, and Sean asked if I needed him to carry Willa, but I lowered her to the ground, saying, *I think I'll be all right.*

We walked gently. By the time we reached the Bartram Forest parking lot, my heart rate had slowed. Sean left to visit with relatives while I took Willa to lunch. Upon driving home, as Willa ran up the walk, I waited in the driveway for the mailman. Lingering there, I felt uncharacteristically impatient; the mailman was taking forever to find a package. Why was he so slow? Finally, with the Christmas gift in hand, I trudged towards the house.

As I stood in the front doorway, the large living room felt unusually small. I said to my wife, Renee, *I need to sit down.* My heartbeat felt rapid, yet it shouldn't have since Willa and I had sat for almost an hour at lunch, and the walk into the house measured less than ten yards. My goal suddenly became trying to reach a brown-cushioned chair.

Easing my body down, I said to Renee, *Feel my heart.*

She placed her hand upon my chest.

Listen to my heart.

She pressed her ear against my shirt, listened, and said, *Your heart is racing.*

Something, I said, *is very wrong.*

I lay upon a couch and soon felt my heartbeat slowing, but I feared the unknown, the gray area of what might be the matter. Since nothing physically hurt now, and since my heart rate remained steady, I decided to wait until morning to see the doctor. Still, I fell asleep worrying about what the doctor would find.

In the morning I drove myself in, and the nurse promptly administered an EKG. Then as I sat anxiously in the exam room, the doctor strode in and asked, *Allen, how long have you been feeling like this?*

You're making me nervous, I said.

Your heart is in a-fib right now, the doctor explained. *It's beating out of rhythm. You need to be driven to the Macon Heart Center immediately to be treated by a cardiologist.*

I telephoned my wife and told her that she needed to drive over with her mother, Margie, and take my truck back to our house before bringing me to Macon, which was forty-five minutes away.

The doctor's receptionist printed out directions and told me I would be Dr. X's patient at the heart center. Renee, Willa, and Margie arrived to take me home. Since my pulse wasn't skyrocketing, I entered the house and packed an overnight bag. I walked slowly, moving carefully, like any sudden move could set my heart off.

The sky was as gray as an anvil, and rain fell steadily as we parked at the Macon Heart Center. When I told the front-desk clerk that my heart was in *a-fib,* she picked up the telephone.

An orderly transported me by wheelchair to room 501. The room had one bed, two chairs, a sofa, light blue walls, and drawn louvered shades. I felt relieved to have my own room but thought that the isolation created a particular solemnity, though whatever a doctor might tell me about my heart shouldn't be overhead by a stranger.

Renee, Willa, and Margie remained in the room as a youthful female nurse told me to change into a standard backless gown. After the nurse attached electrodes to my chest, a tech started an IV. Wires from the electrodes ran to a small transmitter that fit in the front pocket of the gown, and the was transmitter connected to an IntelliVue heart monitor. Within seconds, beeps sounded, and like a condemnation, the words *Irregular Heartbeat* flashed on the heart monitor screen, along with my heart rate, measuring one hundred and twenty-five beats per minute. I felt wary, because my heartbeats didn't feel nearly as fast as when I'd walked into the house the day before. The nurse said I had to remain connected to the heart monitor, and if I urinated it had to be in a plastic pitcher. An IV drip would be started soon, and my blood pressure would be recorded at regular intervals. All told, I felt like a laboratory specimen, the scrutiny stifling, claustrophobic.

Now the nurse questioned me, chronologically reviewing my medical history. I told her my mother's father had died of an aortic aneurism. My father had a heart murmur, a right bundle branch block, and thirteen years ago he'd been fitted with a pacemaker because of fibrillation. I told her my age was fifty and then recited a plethora of surgeries: I'd had my tonsils removed, a broken nose packed and splinted, wisdom teeth taken out, a hernia repaired, and shoulder surgery for bone spurs and a torn labrum. Three weeks earlier, I'd undergone sinus surgery. From my perspective, what the history signified most was that after any medical treatment, my body had always healed or allowed me to resume life freely. I'd suffered no dire consequences. Even after the two months of physical therapy to rehabilitate my shoulder, my doctor had pronounced it functional. In other words, life had been, for half a century, quite benevolent.

The nurse remarked, *Well, you don't look fifty. I'm surprised that your irregular heartbeat didn't show up during the sinus surgery.*

So am I.

I wanted to ask her some questions, but she said, *I have to leave now because it's the end of my shift.*

~

Sifting through my memory, I recalled dragging logs out of the woods a year before. My heart rate had accelerated, but I had believed it was simply because of my approaching fifty, because of my growing old and being out of shape. One March afternoon I had felt like something unknown was slowing my body down while I ran; it had felt difficult to maintain a pace below a twelve-minute mile, but in June and July (prior to injuring an Achilles tendon), I had progressed to five- and six-mile runs at a sub-seven-minute pace. In November I'd felt winded when hauling gravel with a wheelbarrow, resting more than I'd ever needed to. And now, here we were. Apprehension unfurled within me, the realization dawning inside my thoughts, as if a puzzle had finally been solved: my heart had probably been malfunctioning for over a year.

The next nurse was a talkative young man who started rattling off worst-case scenarios: I might require surgery; I might need a pacemaker; tests might show I had suffered a heart attack and damaged my heart muscle; or there could be blood clots in my veins or in my heart.

Do tell, I thought, with pseudo bravado, like a novelist imagining plotlines for characters. But I also felt nervous, as if I'd suddenly peered over a cliff's edge and confronted a perilous drop.

Renee's face had become grave, and I thought that Willa shouldn't have been hearing any serious talk about my health. Margie's face revealed infinite concern.

Soon, a third nurse, a middle-aged woman, entered and informed me that in the morning I would have a transesophageal echocardiography, a sonogram of the heart, the images recorded by a probe inserted down my esophagus. If my heart was free of blood clots, then I would likely undergo a cardioversion. Electrodes would be attached to my chest and back, so my heart could be shocked back into its normal rhythm.

The mood felt ominous; it was as if every molecule in the air had suddenly been altered beyond any state I'd previously known.

Dr. X, the cardiologist, failed to appear by that evening. I told Renee to drive Willa and Margie home because they—or at least she—would need to return in the morning. As my wife kissed me goodbye, I stayed upbeat to ease the departure, reassuring her that I would be all right. But once everyone left, the transmitter attached to my heart stopped working, and the talkative male nurse attached the cables directly to the heart monitor, tethering me to the bed, requiring me to buzz the nursing staff each time I had to get up to use the bathroom. Suddenly I felt shackled and trapped, and I loathed being alone.

Soon the edges around the window louvers dimmed. The room lights were darkened. I tried to sleep, but the heart monitor beeped loudly, reading *Irregular Heartbeat*, my pulse over 130. Shortly, an urgent voice called out repeatedly over loudspeakers: *Code Blue*, followed by a room number and a doctor's name. The sound of hurrying footfalls filled the hallway, and as if I were amongst wild animals in the wilderness, death seemed palpable in the air. Yes, many people entered the heart center and failed to walk out, because the heart was such a fragile organ. What, I wondered, was wrong with mine?

When I tried to relax, my heart rate slowed down to forty beats per minute; the monitor beeped, and *Low Heartbeat* flashed on the screen. I remembered, of all things, being sixteen, running high school cross-country, and having recorded a similar low heart rate for a physical. My heart shouldn't have been able to beat so slowly. At that rate, what was to keep my heart from now stopping altogether?

After midnight my thoughts dragged me down into the most maudlin realm. I felt tired of being stuck in the room and soon became anxious from watching the monitor, knowing that my heart was beating only far below and far above the normal limits. I thought of how it was

Friday and Monday would be Christmas Eve. The night deteriorated into further sleeplessness; I lay in the dark for hours, considering too many worst-case scenarios. My solitude was interrupted by a tech needing to record my vital signs. Soon, a nurse, trying to determine causes of the significant fluctuations of my heart rate, asked if I'd been taking any medications. I answered, *No*, and struggled to fall sleep, feeling trapped in a limbo between this world and the next. I couldn't help thinking of four friends who had died—three from suicide, the other from a heart attack. *Janet, Rob, Dave, and Dave*, I thought, *How are things on the other side?*

The morning nurse, who was Filipino, outdid the other nurses by finding a transmitter that worked, restoring my mobility. Before Renee arrived, an orderly delivered me by wheelchair downstairs, where I was placed on a movable hospital bed for the echocardiography and cardioversion.

A bespectacled nurse prepped me, explaining how I would be given anesthesia, and then the cardiologist, Dr. X, finally appeared. He was pudgy, balding, affable, and came across like a mellow former hippie. *If the first test goes right, we'll shock your heart back into rhythm. Since you'll be asleep, you won't feel a thing. If all goes well, afterwards you'll feel fine.*

If, I thought.

The room felt cold. They anesthetized me, and I went under while being wheeled into another room. When I awoke, Renee was standing by my bed, asking how I felt. *The echocardiography didn't reveal anything more, so they shocked your heart*, she said. *The doctor said it worked.*

For how long? I wondered.

Late that afternoon, Dr. X entered my room and told me that Doctor O would be covering for him for the weekend. He explained that since my heart had been beating out of rhythm, it had gotten out of shape; the condition of my heart on a 1 to 10 scale was now an 8. I worried that my heart might be permanently weakened. Renee commented later that Dr. X hadn't explained what had caused my irregular heartbeat or offered a prognosis. He did mention, however, that I should ask Dr. O a lot questions, joking it would be good for her. When the evening nurse told me that Dr. X was going on vacation like many doctors do during the Christmas week, I realized that for my primary care I had drawn the cardiologist who was halfway out the door.

When the Filipino nurse showed up with pills and informed me that my new medications were to be taken twelve hours apart, in the morning and evening, I intuited with a sharp pang that this wasn't temporary or just for my hospital stay, but it was a permanent regimen, for the rest of my life. What had I done to cause this? Early each day I had to ingest an aspirin; a blood thinner, Pradaxa; and two beta-blockers, Carvedilol and Sotalol. The beta-blockers would keep my heart beating in rhythm, not letting the rate drop too low or soar too high. *We need to monitor you here for a few days,* the nurse said, *to make sure the medications are working.*

A few days? Renee remarked she was glad it was only for that long, but I was frustrated and struggling to not be depressed. Seven pills a day seemed implausible, and I thought my heart had betrayed me. To distract my thoughts, I stood up, padded over to the window, and opened the louvers, hoping to see green grass or a dramatic cityscape. But my eyes were met by the view of a gigantic ventilation unit. I had to crane my neck, straining to see upward, just to catch a glimpse of the smallest rectangle, the grayest patch, of dark gloomy sky.

The afternoon meandered by. Left alone that evening, I contemplated calling friends who lived in Macon. Wouldn't it be great to have a party? To eat barbecue or pizza and attempt to ward off all my dismal emotions? I didn't want to be pitied, though, so I couldn't bring myself to contact anyone.

That night no more heart monitor alarms sounded for a low or high heart rate. Still, I found it difficult to close my eyes—what if the medication failed and I died in my sleep? By morning I had rested very little and wanted to be anywhere else. A middle-aged African-American nurse told me I could shower, so I lingered under hot water, washing away two days' worth of grease and sweat from my hair and pores.

When Dr. O, the second cardiologist, walked in, she stood at the foot of the bed and briefly fixated upon my features. She was a brunette, slightly younger than I. When our eyes met, she glanced nervously downward. I didn't have my wedding ring on and inferred that, of all things, she was attracted to me. I supposed that my being much younger than the typical heart patient made me seem rare or more intriguing. Despite the awkwardness, she told me I might need to stay beyond Tuesday.

The idea of being stranded there through Christmas startled me. I thought of Willa and started to cry, embarrassing tears streaming down from my eyes. Trying to compose myself, I apologized, explaining that I knew my wife was having a difficult time driving back and forth and keeping our house together, and my daughter would be acting out in any number of unknown ways the longer I wasn't at home. *I'm sorry. None of this has been easy,* I said. What little optimism I had left was dwindling away; all I wanted now was to go home. Disappointment about my being married had only flickered across Dr. O's face for a moment, and still trying to gather myself, I told her that there were some questions I needed to ask her about my heart. She acted professionally, telling me, *I'll be back later,* granting me more time to regain my composure.

That afternoon when Renee and Willa arrived, my daughter climbed onto the bed, and I read to her. I became emotional, not wanting to disappoint her, not wanting to tell her that I might not be home for Christmas. *Please, go find something to eat or drink, or ride the escala-*

tors, I said, and by then I was crying. The future had become much too uncertain; I felt emotionally torn asunder. And I thought of how I had always been able to pull on a pair of running shoes, step out the door, and accrue four to six miles without a second thought, simply trusting my limbs and body, but now that confidence had suddenly vanished, as if my freedom had been stolen.

How much of an illusion do most of us live with, I mused, never recognizing the fragility of our health?

By the time Renee and Willa returned, I had composed myself. Dr. O entered the room, and Renee and I asked questions. We learned that I would still be able to exercise, but the doctor recommended not running sub-seven-minute miles. Coffee and Coke or Pepsi were out because caffeine was a stimulant that would contradict the beta-blockers. My irregular heartbeat and atrial fibrillation stemmed from an electrical problem, meaning the bundles around my heart weren't transmitting the proper signals, which was a condition (not a disease) that I couldn't have done anything to prevent. Needing a pacemaker someday couldn't be ruled out.

Still waiting to see if the medication would regulate my heart properly, I felt glum, sorrowful, stuck in the doldrums of midlife. When Renee and Willa left that evening, I nearly cried again, and my eyes focused upon the heart monitor, still tracking the ups and downs, making sure the range didn't dip too low or rise too high, like I was visually tightrope walking. Sleep once again eluded me, and when an orderly served me eggs and bacon that Sunday morning, I wondered if I was really in a heart center or if it was all a mystifying dream. But Dr. O appeared, and to my astonishment informed me that I would be discharged that evening. She explained that as long as I kept up with my medications, I'd be better off not doing any extensive reading about my heart and just living my life for a while. Lastly, she smiled and told me that she was a single parent, as if to say she more than understood raising a child and my reasons for having become so upset.

I telephoned Renee, letting her know about my imminent release, suggesting she drive over in the late afternoon. It was the day before Christmas Eve, so I behaved like a model patient all morning and afternoon, not wanting to endanger my departure. Renee and Willa arrived at four o'clock; an hour later a nurse told me I had been officially discharged. I felt ecstatic, but on the way home when we stopped at a CVS to have my new prescriptions filled, I found myself buying a long plastic pillbox with letters for each day of the week on top of seven compartments. My parents, who were in their mid-seventies, used similar boxes, so I felt discouraged and resented my fate. My concerns about whether my heart would stay in rhythm left me feeling guarded about how happy or content I could truly be. How much was my life my own now? The fact that my own living tissue, the most important muscle in my chest, had rebelled against me, not behaving anymore as it should, felt unfair, like the cruelest betrayal possible.

On Christmas Eve day, I shopped for groceries I'd need for cooking a roast for my family and stayed up late wrapping Renee's and Willa's presents. Christmas was splendid simply because I was at home with my family, and in those initial days I didn't try to run or exercise. The new worst-case scenario would have been triggering a rapid heartbeat and having to return to the heart center. Instead, late at night while Renee and Willa slept, I brooded, watching a slew of B movies, the Robert B. Parker series featuring Tom Selleck as police chief Jesse Stone. I felt comforted by the predictability of each movie. Stone always solved his cases, and whenever an attractive actress was listed in the opening credits, she would always make an overt pass at Stone—those scenes were laughable because of how blunt the actresses were. Most of all, Stone's masculinity always prevailed over criminal attempts on his own life, and he persevered for justice despite his failed marriage or the demons of his own alcoholism.

My medications now kept my heart rate within acceptable parameters, but I could feel the beta-blockers working; an unnatural wave would pass through my chest, slowing and holding back my heart, as if an artificial force or presence were maintaining my life, rather than my own body. I recalled Dr. O saying I'd be better off just living my life, and I knew I needed to attempt to restore my heart's efficiency, so availing myself of the benefits of outdoor exercise, I returned to Bartram Forest two weeks after I had left it.

I jogged ever so slowly for the first quarter mile, passing through rows of pines, and my heart beat steadily, but it was as if a governor had been inserted into my chest, as if my body wouldn't allow me to gasp or breathe too deeply; brakes seemed to have been applied, firmly restricting my level of exertion. So my heart, which had always been strong and pure, was now questioning and hindering me. As I ran further, as much as I wished otherwise, I knew my body had not escaped unscathed, and therefore the experience of being alive, of living itself, was no longer the same. My heart now depended upon a daily dosage of seven pills, so my life wasn't my own, my body not continuing on freely without consequences. I felt it with the lessened capacity of each breath, with each diminished stride; there could have been a giant hand controlling me, like I was just a marionette attached to strings. Then, before I was even halfway through the three-mile loop that I had run countless times before, fate became all too present, telling me that I would never run as fast as I used to. My own death now felt closer instead of far off or unimaginable; there was no escaping mortality. How many years did I have left? Would I be able to accomplish everything I wanted to? Indeed, at some point my heart would stop beating entirely, my life span not my own to determine but bound to the realm of echocardiography. Since then, whenever I have glanced at my watch at my slower mile times, no longer naïve, I have been reminded of that previously unknown fact.

By 2042

Not long ago, on Christmas Eve day at Basseterre, St. Kitts, I found myself embarking on a deep-sea fishing trip, but I worried that the wind and the waves and rough waters might be too much, and that I would embarrass myself with seasickness. I also doubted my physical strength—a year earlier, just after turning fifty, I had been diagnosed with atrial fibrillation, my heartbeats irregular and prone to becoming rapid without medication. And two years before, my right shoulder had required surgery for a torn labrum and bone spur removal. Midlife, I felt, hadn't been very reassuring to me.

Five other people boarded the fishing vessel, a white fiberglass 32-foot Century complete with a tower and outriggers: a skinny, angular, young German couple; an overweight, sandy-haired father in his late forties with his husky, sleepy-eyed, twelve-year-old son; and a rugged, black-haired high school kid with intense blue eyes who hailed from Fort Worth.

We were welcomed aboard by the charter captain, José, and his first mate, Aldo. Soon Aldo cast off the lines, and we set out from the marina at Basseterre, keeping parallel to the island of St. Kitts on a northwest course. The strongest winds soon gathered, jouncing the boat from the stern. Whitecaps became prominent, and as the boat heaved up and down, I realized we were in for an incessantly rough ride and therefore the longest of days. Why had I wanted to go fishing?

~

I had chosen to go, I remembered, because, like an addict, I had once fished weekly while living a mere forty-five minutes from the Gulf of Mexico in Houston, Texas. Since my wife and I now lived in rural Georgia, I rarely saw the sea and had missed being on the water. I had also wanted to test myself, to see how my heart and shoulder would hold up; I wanted, to a certain degree, to defy midlife and retain my masculinity.

As Aldo hosed down the white floor in the stern because our sneakers and sandals had tracked in sand and dirt, I observed he was barefoot. The five other clients and I were sitting in the forward cabin as José explained that we would be trolling, staying above a reef line that ran parallel to St. Kitts. I saw, as well, that José's dark skin was a shade lighter than Aldo's, and the stubble from not shaving for several mornings covered José's chin and jowls. His sunken eyes had the tired look of a man who'd been staring for too long and too hard at the ocean, and his body appeared gaunt, as if he were more skeletal than solid flesh and blood. I also noticed that the boat was equipped with a state of the art Garmin GPS and sonar system, and I listened to the diesel engines throbbing smoothly, propelling us forward at a steady 7.1 mph. José hadn't opened the front cabin window yet, so I smelled the slightest backwash of diesel fumes, which prompted me to remove my sneakers and head out to stand barefoot with Aldo on the open aft section. As I took a deep breath, he nodded, acknowledging my awareness of wanting to avoid the fumes. I tried not to stare at him, but I couldn't help glancing at several long scars marring his forehead. Though he stood shorter than I by several inches, his upper body appeared far stronger than mine; I thought maybe he'd played sports during his youth or had worked construction.

Aldo glanced at my worn Columbia fishing shirt and asked, "You've fished before?"

"I used to go a lot. In the Gulf of Mexico. My friends and I fished out of Galveston, Texas."

"Four and five hours out?"

"Yes," I said, impressed that Aldo knew that it often took that long to reach the oilrigs or the best deep water. "We caught a lot of red snapper, though, or kingfish and cobia. Mahi-mahi and sharks, too."

Aldo shook his head at the inconvenience of having to travel several hours out to fish, and as if expressing additional opposition to the thought, he scaled the starboard tower ladder and began setting an outrigger line, emphasizing how we could start fishing right now, only minutes away from the marina.

Despite the rough day, the Caribbean Sea enlivened me, for the water shone in blue hues unlike any to be found far north. My focus sharpened on our fishing; I glanced into the forward cabin and saw how the Garmin unit registered the water depth at over four hundred feet. Aldo proceeded to set six lines, rigging the hooks with ballyhoo (an ocean baitfish) behind bright, heavy, lead-weighted teasers. Trolling this way could be extremely efficient, because the boat could cover a lot of water; the six baits soon created the illusion of a school of baitfish moving rapidly across the surface, as if they were as if they were vulnerable and fleeing, in distress. But I figured that the rough water and the boat's 7.1 mph speed would not allow the bait to be easily seen by as many big fish or predators as it would if we were trolling slowly through calmer seas.

"Are we going to troll like this all day?" I asked.

"Yes," Aldo answered.

"Then we're going for more of a boat ride than a fishing excursion, aren't we?"

Aldo nodded reluctantly, realizing that I knew their method of fishing amounted to making the time pass more than striving to deliver a bona fide fishing expedition—complete with landing fish—for their clients.

"Do you *ever* anchor up and drop bait, so everyone can catch something?" I persisted.

"No," Aldo said.

I sighed, and the very air seemed to thicken between us, as if suddenly the fact that I had paid for the trip and knew from experience about fishing might become indomitable leverage. But then I said in a relaxed tone, freeing Aldo from being more honorable, "At least we're out here fishing, instead of staying ashore."

Aldo smiled, grateful that I wasn't going to protest about their speedy trolling. My eyes became distracted by the beauty of the green hillsides sloping upward from the shoreline. The hillsides soon steepened, giving way to volcanic mountains, and then the more hospitable shorelines further northwest became dotted with houses of extravagant colors, like Popsicle orange, hot pink, cherry red, cerulean blue, lime green, and canary yellow. We passed the small towns of Challengers and Old Road. Soon the German woman joined Aldo and me on the open aft area; she took a deep breath and tipped her head back, basking in the sun. Her face was youthful and noble, with brown freckles and strong cheekbones, and she wore her long brown hair smoothed back in a ponytail. Her blue eyes shone with exuberance. Hoping to inspire luck, I told her, "You should reel in the first fish."

Aldo agreed with a nod, and then I said, not wanting to appear selfish, and hoping the fishing gods might somehow smile upon me if made some type of personal sacrifice, "I'll go last."

As the German woman grinned nervously at the thought of fighting the first fish, the high school kid from Fort Worth emerged, followed by the father of the twelve-year-old (who was still in the cabin, fast asleep), while the German husband stood beside José, talking about how to operate the boat.

I asked Aldo, "How often do you fish?"

"At least twice a week, man."

"What pound test do you have on the reels?"

"Fifty pounds."

"You set the drags light?"

"Very light, so the lines don't easily break." Aldo glanced ahead and pointed to the port side, where a brown pelican sat in the water like a sentinel, bobbing alone on the waves.

I thought of how birds sometimes waited to feed atop schools of bait, so there could have been large fish below. "Sometimes the smallest thing can mean everything," I said.

Aldo's eyes gleamed, and he wagged his head, saying, "Yeah, yeah."

Aldo whistled at José and pointed at the pelican, so José aimed the bow towards the bird. As the boat drew nearer to it, no fish struck, and when the pelican flew away, José swung the boat back over the reef. Soon he began maneuvering the boat through a series of S turns, crossing back and forth over the reef. Suddenly, a fishing reel whined. Aldo bounded across the aft section. He grabbed the rod from its holder, lifted the rod, reared back, set the hook, and motioned for the German woman to hurry into the fighting chair. She shuffled over and sat down, and Aldo placed the rod in the holder in front of her. Noticing all of the activity, her husband came outside and joined us.

José barely slowed the boat, so the German woman bent down and strained, reeling until a small flash of silver broke the surface. She and her husband laughed, and she grunted, reeling in a silver skipjack that was no more than a foot long. Aldo worked the hook from the fish's mouth, then threw the skipjack into a bucket, reached into a cooler, baited the hook with a fresh ballyhoo, and set the line out again.

We trolled past the town of Half Way Tree. We were approximately six miles from port. There were no more strikes, so the German couple drank several beers, superstitiously sacrificing sobriety to improve the boat's chances. Soon another reel sang as if prompted by the drinking, and as the German couple laughed at their alcohol-induced luck, Aldo called to the husband to occupy the fighting chair. Aldo set the rod in front of him, and the husband put his shoulder into fighting the fish, but it was only another small skipjack. We all sighed, having hoped for a bigger catch.

Beyond Brimstone Hill another reel sounded, and Aldo hastened to the rod, lifted it from the holder, and attempted to set the hook. The fish had stolen the bait, though—there was nothing there—and in my mind I questioned the boat's speed again, but soon another reel buzzed. As Aldo grabbed the fishing rod, the teen from Fort Worth commandeered the fighting chair as though believing that the initiative of his assertion could lead us all to a greater piscatorial reward. He leaned back, brought the rod down, and reeled furiously, but his profound effort only result- ed in yet another small skipjack. The teen's eyes said that he wanted to chastise José and Aldo, as if he, too, knew they were fishing too fast, but then he stood up, held onto the base of the starboard tower ladder, and braced himself as the water grew rougher.

Our surroundings soon felt more ominous; Mt. Liamuiga, a dor- mant volcano (formerly called Mt. Misery) and the highest point on St. Kitts' western side, loomed over us, and frigate birds—resembling pterodactyls because of their long pointed beaks, thin bodies, and tri- angular wings—hovered ahead of the boat and skimmed the waves. The husky twelve-year-old son had been roused by the boat's pitching and crashing through swells, so when a reel on the port side sounded, Aldo called him out to fight the fish. The boy tottered onto the aft deck, struggled into the chair, and within a minute and to no one's surprise, he landed a skipjack. His father said gruffly to me, "You can go next."

"You should follow your son," I said.

"I'm older than you," the father said.

"How old are you?"

"Forty-six."

"I'm fifty-one," I said.

"I don't believe you."

"I can show you my license," I offered.

The father didn't challenge me again. A few minutes later when an- other reel whined, he sat down in the fighting chair without protesting.

He reeled in the fish quickly—it turned out to be yet another skipjack, so he frowned at me, as if blaming me for his poor luck.

I didn't feel the slightest amount of guilt or selfishness for having called the last turn. How could I have known where the boat would be or what the conditions would be like when my turn arose?

We left the island of St. Kitts behind, venturing into much deeper, more open water. All at once, like fighter planes on strafing runs, frigates dove on all sides of us, feeding voraciously on plentiful schools of bait. In the distance to the north, a volcanic island rose up like a foreboding portent, a reminder of the formidable power of nature.

"Dolphin!" Aldo shouted. He gestured urgently to José, and what I saw next were not dolphins like Flipper but the blunt-shaped heads of mahi-mahi, circling below and savagely slashing upward, ambushing bait on the surface. José yanked the wheel and steered the boat to bring the teasers and the ballyhoo closer to the fish, but the maneuver didn't elicit any strikes. Then the boat swung about to keep the wind and waves at the stern, and I watched in sheer awe and horror as a wave rose and its curl grew, the apex extending higher until the crest formed far above my head. The wave appeared like a living entity that wanted to pursue the boat and flip us over. Oh, God, I thought, and at that moment I experienced a feeling that I'd known only a few times before: it was a tingling or a sensation of deeply heightened awareness, my intuition telling me that something significant was about to happen. Indeed, I felt fortunate to be alive now, to inhabit the earth and space and time, as if my life were a part of something far more than midlife alone. Most importantly I knew—despite how I would barely be able to stay in the chair because of the ferocious waves bearing down upon us—that I was about to hook a big fish.

Thirty seconds later, the starboard rod and reel connected to the outrigger screeched; a fish struck and was taking yards and yards of line out, and despite the harshness of the waves, Aldo bounded across the aft section. He was all serious business as I stumbled into the fighting chair, and I laughed at how the prophecy of my intuition had been realized, but I feared whether I could stay in the chair and handle a big fish in such severe water. Still, part of me felt very excited and glad to be there, confronting the extreme challenge. Aldo yanked back on the rod twice, setting the hook. After carefully bringing the rod over and dropping it into the holder, he shouted, "Reel!" I bent over, putting my surgically repaired shoulder into the fight.

José slowed the boat a little. As excited as I felt, my heart did not beat wildly, the beta-blockers for my atrial fibrillation keeping my pulse steady. Perhaps because of this, I was very aware, noticing more than when I had fought fish in the past. I counted the five other fishing lines and saw where they were in comparison to the line attached to the rod and reel in my hands. I noted that the angle of the line attached to the reel I was holding slanted sharply, indicating the fish was deep. The waves gathered and crashed, tossing the boat to and fro, evoking thoughts of the *Kon-tiki*, the *Pequod*, and monsters of the deep. And as Aldo worked to haul in the five other lines, I reeled as he'd instructed. Still, the fish didn't move; I could feel all of its weight and then several strong tugs. "Reel!" Aldo shouted again.

"I'll break the line if I do. The fish is head shaking," I said.

"Stay with it!" Aldo exclaimed, more excited than I was.

The fish remained deep, so I lowered the rod, reeled, and gained a few feet of line, but when I brought the rod back up, the fish veered to the starboard and hung far below, as if wanting nothing to do with being forced to the surface. I sensed the fish was toying with me. Suddenly it sliced through the water and remained directly behind the boat, still far below our wake, and José slowed the boat more. I worked the rod downward, reeling as much line as I could. My right shoulder felt tight, but no tendons popped or snapped—everything held together—and although I wished for Hemingwayesque grace under pressure, I felt more like I was barely surviving, just hanging on.

"Reel! Reel!" Aldo shouted.

I gained a few yards of line.

"This is a big fish," I said. "We have to be patient with it."

A huge wave crested and broke right behind the boat, sending a deluge of water over the rail. Soaked, I shook my head and laughed. What else could happen? The battle progressed but seesawed for twenty minutes; I reeled in some line, the fish took some, but I kept gaining line slowly. As I concentrated, it felt like there was no one else on the boat, like I alone was connected to the fish and the sea, though if I became careless and couldn't stay in the chair, the entire ocean waited to receive me and draw me down to the bottom.

"Bring it in!" Aldo shouted, and I could see he'd become enthralled by the fight, but I noticed he'd forgotten to pull in one of the lines which still had a heavy teaser and a ballyhoo attached to it.

"You have to reel that other line in. I'll slice my line if I cross it," I said.

Realizing his mistake, Aldo lifted the other rod and quickly retrieved the line. Now the path to the boat seemed clear, but I feared that the fish, upon being dragged closer, might swim beneath the boat or cut the line in the propeller. Still, I leveraged the fish by pumping the rod, reeling as much as I could when I brought the rod downward, and in time, the end of the leader (a stronger length of line tied between the bait and the line on the reel) appeared above the water. "There's the leader," I called out, my hopefulness increasing; I believed we might actually bring the fish to the boat.

I reeled without having to lower the rod and gained more line, until suddenly my eyes caught sight of the fish. It was sleek but massive, as long as a kitchen table, the sides bronze and highlighted by lit blue vertical stripes, the head narrowing to a point, the mouth filled with jagged teeth. I recognized it as a wahoo, *Acathocybium solandri*, also known in the Caribbean as *Peto*. The fish easily weighed over a hundred pounds.

To my astonishment, Aldo forced his way in front of me to stand at the rail, and I couldn't see the fish anymore. Worse still, he seemed oblivious to how the rod actually rested on his right shoulder. "What are you doing?" I protested loudly. He awkwardly reached with his left hand for the leader and tried to haul some line in. Then he grabbed down for the gaff with his right hand and suddenly took a wild stab at the fish. The wahoo reacted by initiating a run, diving, and shooting like a little missile to the starboard; in a matter of seconds I felt all of the resistance from the end of the line dissipate, leaving me holding nothing.

I sat there stunned, incredulous, not wanting to believe how badly Aldo's attempt to land the fish had been. He should have waited until I called that the fish was played out, that it was ready. By letting the rod rest on his shoulder, he had removed the rod's ability to function as a shock absorber, providing resistance when the wahoo dove. The fish had been able to yank the hook out of its own mouth because of how Aldo had been forcefully holding onto the leader. I knew all of this from having successfully landed several big fish in the past.

Having paid for the charter, I would have felt justified in yelling at Aldo. I had seen and heard many fishermen berate a boat's crew for mistakes. Aldo had been reckless and incompetent, not to mention how we'd been trolling too fast from the start. I merely shook my head silently, though, as disappointment rived through my mind and filled my entire body. Aldo looked at me, waiting, anxious, wondering, anticipating my severe pronouncement.

The five other clients appeared bothered by the roiling waves and the lack of landing any big fish; they, too, were not happy with José or Aldo. They offered me their consolations as José shut the forward cabin front window and climbed up onto the tower. He began steering from above, turning the boat around so that the bow faced southeast, aiming directly into the wind. The waves broke hard against the bow, drenching the front window; we were heading back to Basseterre. Aldo set out the six lines again, and as we continued to troll—motoring against the wind—we even passed by another boat that was also trolling.

"Aren't we moving too fast to hook anything now?" I said.

Aldo nodded at me with the same begrudging reluctance he'd expressed earlier. "We have another trip this afternoon. Out of Nevis," he said. Since José and Aldo had brought us out for several hours and hooked one large fish, I supposed that, in their minds, they had done enough. But I had been on other fishing trips where multiple hookups were the norm and the expectation, so I felt more upset now about losing the wahoo. I contemplated how, if I had caught it, I would have strained to lift the fish but then held it up, the moment making for a once-in-a-lifetime photographic trophy. I had certainly never caught a wahoo like that before, and I thought of how wahoo fillets are highly praised by gourmands.

"Your fish," Aldo said, trying to save face now, "it ran and lost the hook. Sometimes, there's nothing you can do." His eyes betrayed that he was still fearful of my judgment.

I inhaled deeply to let the clean ocean air calm my thoughts. How long had it been since I'd been deep-sea fishing? I realized that over a decade had passed since I'd moved to rural Georgia and been out on a bigger boat. My eyes swept across the ocean on all sides, absorbing all the variations of blue, and I felt glad that my heart had kept in rhythm and that my shoulder had let me fish again. How often was I given the opportunity to hook a wahoo and do battle? Wasn't I fortunate to have hooked the trophy fish, rather than a skipjack? Hadn't I fought it perfectly, bringing it to the boat, and hadn't I seen it? Yes, a bruiser of a fish, so alive, with all its resplendent colors—it had escaped the hook, but I knew the image of it would not escape my mind. I considered, as well, how Aldo had told me he fished at least twice a week; in comparison, I was an American who worked indoors too much. Then I thought of how, by 2042, minorities in America would likely outnumber whites, and our behavior then, as we traveled abroad, could bring a whole new meaning, or a reversal, to the term Ugly American. I knew I probably wouldn't still be alive by then, but this was like a brief preview of that future time, and I did not want to seem at all like or be an Ugly American, much less an Ugly Chinese-American. How insensitive would I be as a person of color if I berated Aldo, another person of color? How far would I have fallen if I behaved in a stereotypically white way? Shouldn't I prioritize being part of the larger community of the world *right now*, instead of far in the future? I also considered that I would be catching fish like the wahoo more often if my life were arranged differently, which was not Aldo's fault. And that day, once the sun went down, would be Christmas Eve.

I asked Aldo, "Will you be at home with your family this evening?"

"Yeah, man. After the trip to Nevis."

Wouldn't I be a better man, I thought, if I released Aldo, like a fish, setting him free from any bitterness between us, any ill will? "Most fish are lost right at the boat. It's never certain. You did everything right," I lied, adhering to higher moral ground by relieving Aldo of any guilt.

He smiled faintly, relieved that I wouldn't be reprimanding him. I felt better for making the compassionate choice, for having offered a kinder, gentler response.

"Do you own your own boat?" I asked him.

"Yeah. A 16-foot Boston Whaler," Aldo said.

"I have a 17-foot Carolina Skiff. It's about the same."

"I caught a one-thousand-pound black marlin from my boat," he recounted. "It took six hours to haul it in, and the fish towed us far off the island."

I laughed. We swapped a few more fishing stories. Soon José throttled up the diesel engines, requiring Aldo to haul in the six lines and clear the ballyhoo from the hooks. We sped back to the marina, grinding out the last six miles along the coast, lurching violently, the ride far rougher than when we had come out. Everyone looked green, on the verge of seasickness. As we docked, the high school guy from Fort Worth looked like he wanted to pummel José and Aldo for how we hadn't caught anything else, and the overweight father helped his husky son wobble to his feet. Standing arm in arm, the German couple commiserated with each other about the long, rough ride. José and Aldo tried to shake hands with everyone as we stepped ashore, smiling, thanking us for going fishing. But I was the only one who acknowledged them, and I have been contemplating since then about what happened between Aldo and me, wondering about the influence of minorities in what will be a very different America, the world rapidly transforming.

My Chinese-America:
A Meditation On Mobility

ALABAMA

I recently resigned from being the faculty advisor for the Georgia College Bass Fishing Team because of a heavy workload. The sixteen anglers on the team are white Southerners. I boasted about having the best rednecks in Georgia on the water. We were ranked 7th in the nation out of over two hundred and fifty teams. This May, the Boat U.S. Collegiate Fishing Championships will be on Pickwick Lake in Alabama. I would wager a million dollars that I would have been the only Asian-American coach there.

ALASKA

One of my uncles leases a trailer on the Kenai Peninsula for summer salmon fishing. I will visit him if I fly north next year to fish with my longtime friend, the poet Derick Burleson, who teaches at the University of Alaska, in Fairbanks. Due to a feud, my uncle and I did not speak for several years, but we resumed talking last fall for our family's sake.

ARIZONA

In 1972, our family traveled across the country in a Chevrolet station wagon with no air conditioning. Beyond Fredonia, Arizona we stopped at the edge of the Grand Canyon. As I peered out over the northern rim, my eyes strained but couldn't discern the opposite side. I was ten years old; I believe that this was my first experience with the sublime. The distance gave me a sense of the limitlessness of America.

ARKANSAS

Driving south on Rt. 30 in 1992, I felt saddened by the abundance of tarpaper shacks and poor towns, and then I encountered a huge resplendent billboard proclaiming the nearby town of Hope as President Bill Clinton's birthplace. I was struck by the sense of disparity that can be found within America, judging it to be shameful, and now we have the Occupy Wall Street movement, as if my Arkansas experience was a premonition.

CALIFORNIA

After the San Francisco earthquake of 1906, half of my paternal grandfather's brothers and sisters remained in California. The joke within the Gee family was that the less intelligent stayed, while the smarter ones headed to New York. In 1994, with Hollywood production, comedian Margaret Cho attempted to launch *All American Girl*. This would have been the first Asian-American series on network television. Cho is not Chinese-American, but I was rooting for an Asian sister. In the 1980s, Asian-American serial killer Charles Ng was arrested, under suspicion of having killed up to 25 women in northern California. He is, to borrow the term from a cool website, a disgrasian.

COLORADO

In 1999 I adopted a blonde, blue-eyed teenager. When she was a toddler, I had helped to raise her while dating her single mother. In 2004 when my adopted daughter turned eighteen, I flew her to Denver to meet her biological father who had not seen her since she was an infant. My daughter asked, *Aren't you afraid you'll lose me*? I suppose she thought that blood ties and race—his being white, while I'm Asian—might draw her more toward him, but my reply was a cool, calm, *I don't think so.*

CONNECTICUT

I had a girlfriend in college who was from East Granby, CT. While I was visiting her there, we were having sex when her father knocked on the door asking loudly why she was playing one of his jazz records, a Bill Evans album, but he did not barge into the room. The next day, to be blissfully alone, we went hiking in the woods.

DELAWARE

In 1984, Shien Biau Woo was elected Lieutenant Governor of Delaware. By doing so he became one of the highest ranking Chinese-American public office holders in the nation. In 2000, *A Magazine* ranked him the 6th of the 25 Most Influential Asian-Americans. Unfortunately, until then, I had never heard of him.

FLORIDA

For years my wife's family has vacationed on St. George Island. My parents began flying down to stay, also. In the town of Apalachicola, my mother favors the oysters that are brought in fresh from Apalachicola Bay. I like to run my Carolina Skiff and fish for speckled trout with my father-in-law. I drove to Julia Mae's restaurant in Carabelle once and—because he is family—bought my father-in-law three coconut pies. I would like to retire in Florida because of the fishing and the food and the climate.

GEORGIA

I live in Milledgeville, where Asians are 1.5% of the population. After having been here for eight years, there is still the feeling of living in exile. This year The Chin Chens, a new sitcom, is being produced in Atlanta; maybe it will be the first steadily running Asian-American show—Margaret Cho's *All American Girl* was quickly cancelled. My wife's family is from Atlanta; her grandfather was Bobby Lee Dodd, a legendary football coach at Georgia Tech, named for General Robert E. Lee. My wife gave birth two years ago to our daughter, Willa Margie Dodd Gee. We would have named a son Carter Bobby Dodd Gee. That I could be born in the North, migrate to the South, and potentially have a son named for a Confederate general strikes me as astonishing and uniquely American.

HAWAII

The Asian slang name in Hawaii for whites is haole. Asians can make it difficult for whites to live on the islands; I wouldn't want to be part of a cruel Asian majority. In the *Hawaii Five-O* television series that ran from 1968 to 1980, Steve McGarret, played by Jack Lord, and Danny "Danno" Williams, played by Tim O'Kelly, held center stage above Chin Ho Kelly, played by Kam Fong. In the new *Hawaii Five-O* that debuted in 2010, Steve McGarret is played by Alex O'Loughlin, and Danny Williams is played by Scott Caan. Chin Ho Kelley is played by Daniel Dae Kim, and the one addition is Kono Kalakaua played by Grace Park. So now two white men are above an Asian man and a very attractive Asian woman. Progress? Not as long as Asians remain subordinate.

IDAHO

In 1870, over four thousand Chinese-Americans lived in Idaho, constituting over thirty percent of the state's population. The most well-known Chinese-American Idaho pioneer was Polly Bemis, born

Lalu Nathoy in China. She and her husband, Charlie Bemis, helped settle the rugged territory of Idaho along the Salmon River. Despite early anti-miscegenation laws, they were married by a white judge, who was married to a Native-American. I have read that interracial marriage laws were still on the books in South Carolina in 1998 and in Alabama in 2000. The Polly Bemis cabin is listed on the register of national historic landmarks; I would like very much to see it.

ILLINOIS

One of my cousins works for American Airlines. On September 11, 2001, she said quick goodbyes to fellow flight attendants at Logan Airport. Some were bound for Los Angeles on Flight #11 on a Boeing 767. My cousin normally flew that route, but that morning she drew a flight to Seattle. Al-Qaeda terrorists hijacked Flight #11 and at 8:46 a.m. crashed the Boeing 767 into the North Tower of the World Trade Center. My Uncle George was under the impression that my cousin, his daughter, was on Flight #11. Upon hearing that she had been on another flight that morning, he dropped to his knees and wept. My cousin still flies for American. My older adopted daughter, visiting Denver, judged that her biological father tried too hard to act youthful, taking her to a bar although she was only eighteen. Since she still wanted me, as I predicted, to be her primary father, I have visited her regularly in Chicago where she's in graduate school. If I happen to find myself alone, I like to explore the Chicago Institute of Art, intrigued by Georgia O'Keefe's murals that speak of vast spaces, but I am equally drawn to Joseph Cornell's miniaturist boxes.

INDIANA

My older brother attended the University of Indiana's renowned graduate program in music where he studied with Camilla Williams, the first African-American to receive a regular contract with a major American opera company; in 1946, she made her debut with the New York City Opera singing the title role in Puccini's *Madama Butterfly*. My brother visits her in Bloomington whenever possible, as if she is part of our family.

IOWA

I studied at the Iowa Writers Workshop from 1987 to 1989. One morning before a football game, members of a Latino fraternity congregated on the porch of their frat house, appearing strong, rugged, proud, and no doubt at odds with the prevalent whiteness of the Midwest, all too conscious of the constant stigma of their otherness. They saw me, a fellow person of color, walking by, and gave silent nods of respect. In 1991, twenty-eight-year-old astronomy and physics student Gang Lu killed four Iowa faculty members and one student and seriously wounded another student before committing suicide. Lu was infuriated because his dissertation did not receive the prestigious D.C. Spriestersbach Dissertation Prize. One of my mentors remarked that academia is now Asian turf, in the same way that African-Americans have street credibility.

KANSAS

In Kansas a state trooper pulled me over on a remote highway claiming that I hadn't used my turn signal to change lanes. He interrogated me and requested to search my vehicle, suspecting I was running drugs because of my Texas license plates. When the trooper searched through my books from the University of Houston library system, along with my running clothes, his jaw clenched furiously over his not finding anything. I told him—referring to the old anti-drug public service announcement on television showing a frying egg—that my brain was not on drugs and that my best friend from high school is a state trooper. We stood beside my truck in the middle of vast Kansas farmland, reluctance dominating the trooper's eyes as he told me without any apology that I should be on my way.

KENTUCKY

I drove my wife once to a literary festival in Bowling Green to support her first book tour. I rarely feel leisurely and often speculate about how much of an immigrant's work ethic has been instilled in me by my parents. But after the festival, like typical tourists, my wife and I visited Mammoth Cave. There was a moment when the tour guide asked for every light source to be extinguished. My wife held my hand as we stood there silently amidst thirty other people in the cave's darkness, who like us were trying to be considerate of something larger than ourselves. I have since asked myself, how elusive is the America ideal of freedom for all? Is this ideal too unrealistic to be upheld?

LOUISIANA

On October 17, 1992, Yoshiro Hattori, a sixteen-year-old exchange student, was on his way to a Halloween Party in Baton Rouge. He walked up a driveway to ask for directions and was shot and killed by Rodney Peairs, who believed Hattori was trespassing with criminal intent. At first police declined to press charges, but after intervention by the governor and the New Orleans Japanese consul, Peairs was charged with manslaughter. He was acquitted but later found liable in civil court. This sort of incident leaves a region with a violent scar, making many Asians wonder if we should ever go there. But in the spring of 2000, on the way to the New Orleans Museum of Art, I met and shared a taxi with the woman who is now my wife.

MAINE

In the early 1930s, my grandfather rode by train up from New York City and vacationed along the coast at Kennebunkport and Old Orchard Beach. Everyone else was white. How did he feel entering a hotel lobby or a restaurant? Ordering a lobster or taking a swim? My grandfather once told my father, "America is too big for Chinese to stay only in Chinatown." He left behind black and white photographs of his trips to Maine; he looks like a young tiger, dressed in a suit, cradling a hat in one hand, his face bold and defiant, recklessness gleaming in his eyes.

MARYLAND

In 1991, I attended a wedding on the Chesapeake Bay. During the ceremony, for that small space of time, as a Baptist preacher and a Rabbi wed two of my friends, the world felt moving and harmonious. The following day, friends of the bride hosted a crab feast at the edge of a great swath of lawn, and one's eyes could catch glimpses of the water in the distance, of light refracting off waves. In the hosts' home, I encountered Remington sculptures of horses, cowboys, and Native-Americans. Wealth and patriotism seemed intertwined. I wondered if, as a minority in America, I would ever be able to feel such a deep and openly expressed love of country.

MASSACHUSETTS

In 1981 during my freshman year of college, while courting an intelligent green-eyed brunette, we traveled to Fanueil Hall Marketplace in Boston. She had already kissed me more than once, but that day a fraternity pledge, a young white man, ran towards us, claiming he had to kiss thirty women for his initiation. Before the young woman I was with could object, the pledge was forcing a kiss. She told him to stop, and when I pushed him away, he glared at me with the hatred of privilege and entitlement, an expression that said he had a right to her, but who did I think I was? Once you have encountered an expression like this, you never forget it.

MICHIGAN

My brother and I met last year in Detroit to watch the Lions play the Vikings, as it was supposed to be quarterback Brett Favre's last game. We were warned by the concierge at our hotel not to walk on the nearby streets at night; Motor City's automobile economy had been ailing, so crime rates were high. I thought of how the American road trip—which I had lived for as a teenager—was becoming a passion of the past. We lived frivolously back then, as if oil and gasoline were inexhaustible. Which is worse? What should remain the same? Still, I hoped for better times for Detroit.

MINNESOTA

For several years, I have joked with the African-American poet Sean Hill about flying up and going ice fishing with him in Bemidji, Minnesota. I learned while growing up to ice fish on lakes in the Adirondacks where the ice becomes more than four feet thick. That I could be an Asian-American teaching an African-American how to ice fish in a state first settled by Dakota, Ojibwa, and Ho-Chunk (Winnebago) tribes, with claims of early Norse exploration, that was later inhabited by the French, strikes me as a uniquely American occurrence that should be celebrated or mourned with a whiskey flask.

MISSISSIPPI

In August of 2005, Hurricane Katrina destroyed the house of one of my high school classmates, Sue Chamberlain, in Bay Saint Louis. After living in a FEMA trailer, she finally began rebuilding. The majority of insurance companies, however, ruled damages in the town were caused primarily by flooding and not from a hurricane, and almost no one carried flood insurance. So Bay Saint Louis remained a fragment of what it once was. In 2011, North Beach Food and Spirits was the first waterfront restaurant to reopen. Is six years too long to rebuild? Intending to visit and spend some of my income to support the recovery, I feel guilty for not yet making the trip.

MISSOURI

Once while I was flying, my plane was forced to land in Kansas City due to a raging snowstorm. The slender brunette sitting beside me asked with a smile if I wanted to share a hotel room. I remember checking in, but whatever else occurred is a blur of lost details, like time that never was. We didn't exchange names or telephone numbers, and now I have experienced the phenomenon of straining to recall what happened and knowing what must have happened. . .and asking myself, was that really me?

MONTANA

When I flew to Missoula in 2001 to present at a conference, Derick Burleson connected me with the poet Greg Pape, who took me fly-fishing. Snow and ice covered the riverbanks, but my eyes detected rainbow trout. Although Greg coaxed some of them to strike with a wet fly, I did not catch a single fish. Since I lived in the crowded city of Houston at the time, I felt utterly grateful just to be outside, hiking through woods beside running water, and casting a line, and I felt hopeful for how generously I had been shown the territory by someone who was, until then, a complete stranger.

NEBRASKA

One notable Chinese-American Nebraskan is Edward Day Cohota, who joined the Union Army in 1864 and fought in the Civil War. He eventually settled at Fort Niobrara near Valentine, Nebraska, marrying a Swedish-American woman and fathering six children. He died in 1935, ninety years after emigrating from Shanghai. Cohota's story reminds me of my paternal grandfather, Frank Gee, who served in the United States Army. Why do the politicians who rail against immigration never mention all the minorities who have served in the military? Too much of politics has always been self-promoting falsehood and manipulation.

NEVADA

In the 1860s, Chinese-American laborers built the Central Pacific Railroad, leveling the grade and laying track through the high Sierra Nevada territory. For the past decade, Chinese-Americans have been resettling in Las Vegas, their migration fueling ethnic diversity in a city that has long been overwhelmingly white. Ten years ago, Las Vegas' Chinatown was less than three blocks long; today it stretches for almost four miles along Spring Mountain Boulevard.

NEW HAMPSHIRE

I attended the University of New Hampshire, where I was one of less than twenty-five minorities on a campus of over ten thousand students. One weekend, though, during my freshman year, I hitch-hiked from Durham to Woodsville on the Vermont border. John Roy and I arrived at his hometown in the dark. We were welcomed at a bar, and everyone treated me like I was family; I drank for free and danced with young white women the entire night. Several whispered passionately into my ear that they had never seen or spoken with a Chinese-American before meeting me.

NEW JERSEY

Long ago, my grandfather invested in a restaurant in New Jersey with two partners but discovered that they weren't paying him his fair share of the profits. He brought the matter to the Gee Family Association, a tong, in Chinatown, New York. The tong declared that the two partners had to refund my grandfather's entire investment, and that the two men were never to do business with any of the Gee family again. Eventually, I discovered that my grandfather was one of the earliest founders of the tong; at the Gee Family Association building, I was welcomed like a long lost relative and saw my grandfather's name on a metal plaque at the top of a commemorative wall.

NEW MEXICO

My close friend, Renata Golden, now lives in Santa Fe. I have been intrigued by how much the city promotes the arts, including an annual summer jazz festival. I also hear that there are Chinese-Mexican fusion restaurants in New Mexico. Frontier Airlines flies from Atlanta to Albuquerque, and from there one drives to Santa Fe; this is the route I will take to visit Renata.

NEW YORK

I was born in Astoria, Queens and lost what Cantonese I could speak when my family moved to Albany. My parents insisted on my becoming fluent only in English because it was what was needed most to succeed. On April 3, 2009, Jiverly Wong entered the American Civic Association's immigration center in Binghamton, where he shot and killed fourteen people, himself included, reportedly because of his feelings of being "disrespected" for his poor English speaking abilities, as well as frustration over unemployment. Current immigration detractors overlook New York's Chinatown, a thriving community where immigrants work, pay taxes, and uphold family values. Detractors focus instead on those like Jiverly Wong and the burden of costs associated with illegal immigrants. It's rarely stated that America is historically comprised of immigrants, and that, since only Native-Americans can claim that they were here first, my Chinese-America is, in fact, a colonizing American empire.

NORTH CAROLINA

This spring, I visited abstract painter Terrell James on Bald Head Island off the coast near Cape Fear. The island is reached only by ferry or private vessel. Electric golf carts are the only means of transportation on the island. This immediately relieves all residents and vacationers of the stress of traffic jams or the fear of serious accidents. I have vowed to return to the island for a working vacation within five years. I was the only Asian adult that weekend on the island, but I did see a young adopted Asian girl with white parents.

NORTH DAKOTA

There is a place in North Dakota called Chinaman Coulee, a valley five hundred and sixty-four meters above sea level in Williams County. I imagine the history of how Chinaman Coulee was named has been buried deeply, like a corpse. Chinaman Lake, by the way, can be found in Minnesota; Chinaman's Cove in Montana; and Chinaman's Bluff in New Zealand. So not only are there national racist appellations, but there are global derogatory names that nonetheless reveal Asian mobility.

OHIO

In the early 1990's, I veered east to Troy, Ohio to visit an old friend, a Baptist preacher, who asked if I wanted to go sailing on Lake Loramie. Heading north, we stopped at a gas station, and he ran in and bought cigarettes and beer because he felt free to smoke and drink with me, but never in front of his parishioners. That day we hurtled back and forth across the lake with the strongest winds, smoking and drinking like neither of us could ever die. We are both, I'm glad to say, still alive.

OKLAHOMA

I interviewed at Stillwater to teach at Oklahoma State. The eventual hire was the late poet and National Book Award winner, Ai. She described herself as half-Japanese, Choctaw-Chickasaw, Black, Irish, Southern Cheyenne, and Comanche. She had changed her name from Florence Anthony to Ai, which means love in Japanese. Upon hearing she was the hire, I realized the job could never have been mine. I have always associated Oklahoma with humility.

OREGON

An ex-girlfriend from west Texas loves the sun but now lives in Eugene. I hope she isn't depressed by all the rain. She told me once that every man she had dated married right after breaking up with her. As it turned out, she married the next man she dated after me. I told her how glad I was to have helped disrupt her unfortunate pattern.

PENNSYLVANIA

When I was twelve, our family toured Hershey Park; the factory still allowed people to walk close to the gigantic chocolate-filled vats. Now the tour utilizes glass windows. We ate at an Amish restaurant where all of the dishes were served on heaping platters or in large bowls, and this communal way of dining struck me as similar to how

Chinese families share food at banquets, or have *dim sum,* the experience persisting in spite of America's exaggerated emphasis on rugged individuality.

RHODE ISLAND

I have always wanted to write at a place like the Block Island Sound. I hold onto a romanticized image of writing in inspired solitude, by the sea; I would also love to stay at the Panther Orchard Writers Retreat in Hopkington. But I am married with two daughters, and, placing family first and foremost, won't ever be away from my wife or children.

SOUTH CAROLINA

My Uncle Ed's best friend from the Army, Dave Geyer, lived in Greenville. When my Uncle Ed and Aunty Audrey brought me to the Adirondacks to fish, I fished in a boat with Dave. We all met each spring for over twenty-five years. Dave bought a house on Lake Secession in South Carolina but succumbed to heart failure nine years ago. His widow offered to sell me his lake house, so I drove there last spring with a key she had sent me, but the key didn't work. Not being able to see the inside of the house was like not being able to see Dave; standing alone at the front door, I felt the echo of a profound sense of loss.

SOUTH DAKOTA

While traveling toward South Dakota, you can see signs advertising Wall Drug hundreds of miles away. During our family's cross-country trip of 1972, turning into the Wall Motel parking lot, we were greeted by "Welcome to the Gee family!" in huge block letters on the motel's front sign. My father wondered aloud if they knew we were

Chinese, but the front desk clerk didn't show the slightest trace of surprise when we checked in.

TENNESSEE

My wife's grandfather grew up in Kingsport and played quarterback at the University of Tennessee, where he was named an All-American. We have never been to Kingsport or Knoxville but would like to make a football pilgrimage. I have wondered if any Chinese-Americans visit the Grand Ole Opry in Nashville. I favor the improvisation of jazz and can't quite see myself becoming a country music fan.

TEXAS

I lived in Houston for a decade and discovered a Gee Family Association and two Chinatowns. I frequented one restaurant, Canton Seafood, and ate *dim sum* at *My Kahn* each month with Asian friends. Houston is where I learned about the souped-up, ultra-fast aesthetic behind Asian-owned cars called rice rockets, and I watched Yao Ming play center for the Houston Rockets. The city became my second home. I lived with my wife for two years in Houston, and because of that time, I knew that she was the one.

UTAH

My older brother lives in Salt Lake City; to our family's disbelief, during high school he rejected the Methodist church and became a Mormon. In the 1990s, he played a concert at the Mormon Tabernacle. My family was seated beside the Prophet, the Mormon equivalent of the Catholic Pope. My mother insisted that we move closer to the stage so she could see my brother's hands when he played the piano; prioritizing our Chinese-American family, she was not concerned about our offending the Mormon congregation or the Prophet. So we left the Prophet in his row further back.

VERMONT

I visited a woman in Burlington after having confessed that I had a crush on her. On the first evening we found ourselves in a bar, dancing closer than we had ever been. When we returned to her house afterward, nothing happened—the chemistry was missing, or maybe fate had deemed we stay apart. I felt for the remainder of my single days that no matter where one travels, love is never certain.

VIRGINIA

In April, 2007 at Virginia Tech, Seung-Hui Cho, who had been diagnosed with a severe anxiety disorder, killed thirty-two people and wounded twenty-five others before shooting himself. After the tragedy, white people in my small town glanced at me warily, as if I could be capable of murder by association. What was it about America that drove Cho to become a lone gunman? How much was race a factor, in addition to our violent culture?

WASHINGTON

Long ago, I flew to Seattle and then drove to Vancouver in a rental car for a date with an old girlfriend who had sent me flirtatious pictures of herself. The drive along Highway 5 was stunning, the views of the Pacific enlivening, like a calling or a temptation. Indeed, I wanted to live on the coast, to always be swimming, surfing, or fishing, but the date turned out disastrously. I live far inland now and sometimes wonder how free we really are to be where we would like. How limited are we by our lack of initiative?

WEST VIRGINIA

West Virginia has the lowest population of Asian-Americans in the country. In a recent Gallup Poll ranking emotional and physical health and 'life evaluation', West Virginia was revealed to be the un-happiest state, scoring lowest. Correlation: dearth of Asian-Amer-icans equals unhappiness? On Oct. 21, 2010, John Raese, the West Virginia Republican Senate Candidate was caught on film making fun of Chinese-American Secretary of Energy, Dr. Stephen Chu. Raese claimed he didn't know if Chu's name was Dr. Cho, Dr. Chow, or Dr. Chow Mein. Perhaps West Virginia shouldn't be a priority to visit, but I'll make my own judgments from being there.

WISCONSIN

One May, a group of friends and I convoyed to Madison to run a marathon. On the day of the race, the temperature soared into the nineties; none of us hit our desired times. Afterwards we drank beer on the University of Wisconsin's giant patio overlooking Lake Men-dota. As I felt the sun on my face and a whisking breeze and shared pitchers with friends, and as the alcohol numbed my sore limbs, there could be no better sense of leisure, my immigrant work ethic completely forgotten.

WYOMING

In September of 1885 in Rock Springs, white miners burned down the Chinese quarter, murdering twenty-eight Chinese. No one was prosecuted, the massacre serving as a precedent for further an-ti-Asian attacks. President Grover Cleveland, though appalled by the violence, later concluded that because of how anti-Chinese prejudice was so deeply entrenched in the West, and because of how Chinese and American cultures were so different, the Chinese would never be assimilated. I have crisscrossed the country for desire, love, education, family, work, and to fish, vacation, and explore history, trying to see America for its breadth and its smaller intricacies, never straying towards violence. Remembering the Latinos on the front porch in Iowa, I think of how immigrants still struggle to move here to America, hoping for freedom, and I wonder: since I have experienced mobility, why shouldn't others?

Acknowledgments

I'd like to thank these editors for helping to improve these essays and for first bringing them into print: Allison Joseph, Carolyn Allesio, Tim Fredrick, Carol Reposa, Paul Guillen, Juan Pablo Plata, Laura Wallach, Kendra Rajchel, Sophia Plaf Shalmiyev, Jennifer Acker, Rose Blouin, Lacey Dunham, and Richard Hoffman.

My deepest thanks to Andrew Gifford and the judges and editors and staff at Santa Fe Writers Project for selecting this book and for all their work on its publication.

I'm grateful to my colleagues in the English and Rhetoric Department. Georgia College provided a semester of professional leave, which allowed me to spend invaluable time with all of these essays. A special thanks to Alex Blazer, Megan Melancon, John Sirmans, Beauty Bragg, Katie Simon, and Bruce Gentry for talking the talk with me. To Marty Lammon, Laura Newbern, Alice Friman, and Peter Selgin in the creative writing program, you are terrific to work with.

I remain indebted to my agent, Gail Hochman, and to Colin Kennedy and Bettie Cartwright for their guidance and support during my time in Houston. There are teachers who have been the most meaningful influences: Thomas Williams, John Yount, Sarah Sherman, Elaine Ognibene, James Alan McPherson, Joan Chase, Rosellen Brown, Kathleen Cambor, Chitra Divakaruni, and Lawrence Hogue. And to John Marks, James Hynes, Anthony Farrington, Rich Levy, Terrell James, Sean Hill, Renata Golden, Derick Burleson, Laura Long, Amy Hassinger, Mark O'Connor, Sara Cortez, Misty Matin, Melissa Studdard, James Langston, Mike Woodson, Dan Bauer, and Emmanuel Little: I deeply value our friendships.

I'd like to thank my extended family, especially Edward and Audrey Moy, Dave Geyer, Cho-Young Kim-Wiles, John Moy, Myrna Moy, George and Lei-Jayne Moy, May Gee, Lawrence, Brian, Monica, and

Cathy Gee, and also Margie Dodd, Bobby Dodd Jr., Anne Ballard, Jillian Armenante, and Alice Dodd. And of course my children, Ashley and Willa, and my wife Renee, without whom none of this would be worthwhile or possible. And finally, this book is for my parents, Eugene and Lucy, who have seen me through everything.

About The Author

Allen Gee is a graduate of The University of New Hampshire, the Iowa Writers' Workshop, and The University of Houston. He is currently an associate professor of English at Georgia College, where he teaches in the M.F.A. program.

A NOTE FROM THE PUBLISHER

Thank you for purchasing this title from the Santa Fe Writers Project (**www.sfwp.com**).

I started publishing because I love books. I publish titles that I would buy, and that I want to see on the shelves, regardless of genre. SFWP's mission is not about creating a catalog that the accountants can get behind. The mission is one of recognition and preservation of our literary culture.

I encourage you to visit us at www.sfwp.com and learn more about our books and our mission.

Happy reading!

Andrew Nash Gifford
Director
@sfwp

Santa Fe Writers Project

31901056162136